The Mother of All Meltdowns

Real Stories of Moms' Finest (Worst, Completely Awful) Moments

SIGNATURE REVIEWS

"Do you ever find yourself wondering if you are the only one who doesn't react to all situations like June Cleaver? Are there days as a mother where you wish *you* could throw yourself to the ground and have a toddler-style tantrum because you.just. can't.take.it.anymore? Well, so have the thirty hilarious bloggers of The Mother of All Meltdowns! These ladies tell it like it is.

Gone bonkers because your child didn't appreciate the expensive, theme park vacation you booked to make their childhood complete? Check. Lost your cool because your child decided to play barbershop using her own head? Yep, they have been there. Ever punish your child for not eating the lunch you accidentally forgot to make him? They feel your pain.

We could not have enjoyed The Mother of All Meltdowns more … partly because we laughed so hard while reading, we could legitimately skip our abs workout for the week! Score! Every mom reading will come away feeling like she has thirty new girlfriends who just "get it!" All moms deserve the laughter and validation The Mother of All Meltdowns delivers!"

—Lisa and Ashley (a.k.a. The Dose Girls),
The Dose of Reality

"We've all been there. Whether you've had a meltdown or witnessed your child or another in the throes of one, any mom can relate to the universality of the experience. It's easy to feel alone, crazed, or even mortified in the moment, but as proud mothers, we rise above and do what we are often compelled to do—share. The Mother of All Meltdowns is a smart, honest collection by bloggers who tell it like it is, or as we sometimes wish it was. Parenting, warts and all, is celebrated, questioned, and laid bare. You'll chuckle or cringe with recognition, and it's a thoughtful, amusing read for the weary. So, make a cup of tea, carve out some well-deserved downtime, and curl up with The Mother of All Meltdowns. It's a page-turner that will have you smiling!"

—Robin Gorman Newman, Founder, *MotherhoodLater.com*, **Associate Producer,** *Motherhood Out Loud* **and author,** *How to Marry a Mensch*

*This book is dedicated to our children, who most
days melt our hearts, not our brains.*

CONTENTS

A NOTE TO OUR READERS

The Mother of All Meltdowns is a collection of stories written by thirty women—thirty women with very diverse writing styles and blogging techniques. Although we have tried to maintain consistency in grammar, spelling, and stylistic elements, there are some instances where certain writing "components" have been kept intact in order to preserve the authentic voices of the writers.

If you're a word nerd, the grammar police, or anything in between, a good dose of Prozac might be in order before you read this book. We're not about perfection. We're about sharing brutally honest stories in the best way we know how.

So take a few deep breaths, kick your legs up, and read with ease! Life is too short to get caught up on the particulars!

A "meltdown" is ...

Meltdown: noun, def. 1) adult tantrum 2) regressing to the chronological age of three 3) having no ability to express oneself rationally or make a logical case for oneself 4) believing that one's sense of self is compromised or in great danger 5) resorting to slash and burn tactics to try to get needs met

Synonym: fit, bad temper, eruption, hysteria
Antonym: calm, mature, reasonable, thoughtful

When the proverbial shit hits the fan and you are standing there going, "What in the world just happened here?!"

Losing the capacity to think rationally with intermittent dreams of sitting in a bubble bath filled with vodka.

Completely losing it ... emotionally!

Losing it to the point of tears or screaming or inability to progress in the situation!

Becoming hysterical, preferably with laughter, but most often with tears (and not the good ones)!

When logic and reason completely leave you, replaced by raging emotions and, for a moment, you step outside of your body to see yourself and cannot believe the actions you are taking.

When you reach the point of no return as a mom. For me it almost always involves cursing ... a lot.

Completely losing it. Usually involves tears, yelling, and wanting to run away to a far off land. With wine.

Vision clouds, voice rises in volume and pitch, rational thinking ability completely lost. Only my children can reduce me to a puddle of mommy goo.

Feeling so completely overwhelmed by a situation that for a moment you lose all ability to filter your actions and simply let it fly—emotions, frustration, anger, tears. It's the adult-mommy version of a two-year-old kicking screaming temper tantrum. Sometimes that pressure release is all you need to return to the calm, rational mother you know that you are. Other times you're so embarrassed and mortified by your actions, guilt takes over.

It's called a meltdown because you can actually watch your kids melt. They start out upright and solid, then something happens (like juice in the wrong color cup) and they melt; sometimes in slow motion, until they are a puddle on the floor. All wet from screaming and crying, totally immovable.

Introduction

Motherhood. It's often painted in soft colors with lullabies serving as the background music. As butterflies dance and flowers bloom, we—the mothers of the world—are depicted as angels. We can do no wrong. We are the nurturers. The protectors. The ones who make everything better. Our kisses heal wounds that no doctors can fix, and our soothing voices calm even the most hysterical of children.

Despite the demands, the never-ending firestorm of requests thrown upon us, we have the uncanny ability to maintain our composure as proper, love-wielding ladies. Ladies who never … EVER … lose their cool.

You have got to be &$%#@&$ kidding me.

Motherhood is anything but a rosy fairy tale filled with edible rainbows and opera-singing unicorns. This, my friends, is not *Little House on the Prairie*. In fact, motherhood more closely resembles a three-ring circus erected in the middle of a war zone. We are the artillery strapping, man-eating, trapeze artists.

At times, we are so far from angelic, we make Attila the Hun look like Mother Teresa. There is no perfection. There is no walk in the park. Mothers know this. Fathers suspect. The rest of the world, however, sits in denial hoping that the stories of rapture and wretchedness are false.

They're not.

You should be scared.

Very, very scared.

You see, every mother, at some point, inevitably becomes her own worst enemy. In a millisecond, her halo crumbles and she has a moment so crazed it is forever known as the one—

The Mother of All Meltdowns.

The following anthology was written by women who have had their moments. Together we have experienced the anguish and frustration of the adult-sized tantrum. We have shed the tears, dropped to our knees in agony, and asked the age-old question, "Why me?"

From poop-decorated rooms to having our liquid gold scrutinized and confiscated by TSA, we're not afraid to share our collection of thirty tell-all stories. We are survivalists and know that within every meltdown there *is* a silver lining.

So pour yourself a glass of wine, curl up in your favorite comfy chair, and enjoy a little motherly mayhem on us.

If you're a mom, you've definitely earned it.

Crystal Ponti - MommiFried

Not According to Plan

By Lisa Witherspoon
The Golden Spoons

We all know that motherhood does not come with an owner's manual. There is no blueprint, no step-by-step guide to handling different situations. You can read all the parenting books in the world, but there is no way you can prepare yourself for every aspect of being a mom. Every mother's experience is different as well. If you're lucky, you will have supportive people helping you through the struggles and tough times. No matter how much support you have though, motherhood can be hard, and I think meltdowns are inevitable. In fact, my *mother of all meltdowns* happened when I was barely even a mother!

Let me start by giving you a little history.

You know those women who truly just glow when they are pregnant? They gain just the right amount of weight and only in their perfectly round basketball-like bellies. They somehow find all the most fashionable maternity clothes or manage to continue wearing some non-maternity clothes through their entire pregnancies. Maybe they even rock stilettos well into their final months. They seem to have tons of energy, and they use that energy to decorate nurseries that look like they came straight from magazines. They have pregnancy portraits done and look like perfectly-coiffed supermodels. Have you ever met one of those women? Are *you* one of those women?

Well, I was *not* one of those women. With each of my pregnancies, I gained about fifty pounds. I had swollen feet, swollen fingers, and a swollen face. I was wearing maternity clothes about three months in and for a good three months after. I didn't dare let anyone take photos of my grotesquely gigantic self. I was huge. I was uncomfortable. I was tired. I was miserable.

With that in mind, let's rewind to the summer of 2002 when I was nearing the end of my first pregnancy. It was July. I was hot and swollen and grumpy. My due date simply could not come soon enough. Since I was a teacher, I was out of school for the summer. I had pretty much nothing to do but sit around and wait for my labor to start and for that baby to arrive. However, that baby had other plans.

Starting a couple weeks before the actual July 30 due date, I did everything I could possibly do to get that baby to come out. I ate spicy food. Every hot July evening after supper, my hubby and I walked around our neighborhood. I did jumping jacks. (I'm not kidding!) Apparently, that baby was just as stubborn then as she is now because no matter what I tried, she would not come out. To top it all off, somebody—a friend, a relative, a neighbor—checked in every single day to ask, "Anything happening?" Of course, the answer was always, "Nope!" It felt like they were rubbing salt in my wound.

Finally, when I was ten days overdue—a full week into an entirely different month from my supposed due date—my doctor agreed to induce labor. My parents came to spend the night, and we called everyone to let them know that the baby's eviction notice had finally been served! The next morning we were all set to head to the hospital bright and early. Only the hospital called and said they had so many women who actually went into labor overnight, they didn't have a bed for me and that we would have to wait a couple more hours. Seriously. A few hours later, we got checked into the hospital and assigned a delivery room at last.

As with all babies, especially first babies, excitement and anticipation were at an all-time high. We had chosen not to find

out the gender ahead of time which only added to the impatience everyone was feeling. Lots of family members were waiting at the hospital, and everyone wanted to meet this baby.

Like most first-time parents, we had done the childbirth classes and I was prepared, or so I thought. I knew all about the stages of labor. I knew all about the water breaking and the pushing that I would have to do. I also knew beyond a shadow of a doubt that I did *not* want an epidural. You see, I don't get along well with needles, and the idea of someone sticking a giant needle directly into my spine was terrifying. I also have a pretty high tolerance for pain, so I was sure I could endure the labor without the epidural.

Well, the title of this piece is *Not According to Plans,* right? About halfway through the labor process, I did ask for some drugs, but I repeatedly turned down the epidural. Eventually, the drugs wore off, and I continued to suffer through about twelve hours of excruciating back labor. It was nothing like what I learned in childbirth classes or what I had read about in all those books.

Eventually, after being examined *again,* the nurse informed me that I had finally made it to seven centimeters and that this was my very last chance to get the epidural. It was now or never!

Desperate for relief, but still terrified of the needle, I asked the nurse if she had any idea how much longer it would take. I'm sure in her mind she thought that was a ridiculous question, but she kindly responded by saying, "Honey, there really is no way to know. It could be one hour or it could be six. Or, it could be even longer. We just don't know."

Pretty much all I heard was "six hours." "Or longer." Six hours? Or longer?

That's when the mother of all meltdowns happened.

I lost it. I was overcome with all the emotions of that day and the nine months leading up to that day. The weight of the joy, the fear, the excitement, and the discomfort finally became too much for me to bear.

As I sat on the side of that hospital bed, my exhausted body started to shudder and I began to sob. I cried a hard, desperate, and really ugly cry.

As tears streamed down my face, I began tossing a barrage of unnecessary apologies toward my husband. "I'm so sorry, but I don't think I can do this for six more hours! It hurts more than I thought it would, and I am so tired! I am so scared of the epidural needle, but I just have to because I cannot do this any longer! I'm sorry. I'm really sorry!"

In my mind, this meltdown showed that I was not as strong as I should have been—or perhaps as strong as I thought I was. My husband, however, never thought that. Although he hadn't been the one with a baby in the womb, he had also been waiting and anticipating. He had walked with me night after night. He had been to almost all of my doctor appointments. He had watched me in pain for those twelve hours. He had held my hand and rubbed my aching muscles. In that moment, as I buried my face in his chest, he simply held me and let me cry it out. He assured me that it was okay for me to want the epidural and that everything would be all right. Eventually, my crying subsided. The meltdown had given me the emotional and mental release I needed. With the encouragement and comfort from my husband, I was able to regain my composure (as much as a woman in labor can have "composure"). I was once again ready to move on to the next step and, hopefully, closer to delivering this baby.

A little while later, the anesthesiologist arrived. My husband, my one source of calm amidst my turbulent state of mind, stood in front of me. He supported me—literally and figuratively— and before I had another contraction, it was done. Despite my big meltdown and my fear of the enormous needle, the epidural turned out to be no big deal. Compared to the labor pains, I barely even felt it.

Of course, it took a few minutes to take full effect, but once it did, all I felt was relief. Sweet relief. After twelve hours of

contractions and misery, I was finally able to get somewhat comfortable as my body relaxed, no longer in pain. Apparently this was *exactly* what I needed, physically, because less than an hour after receiving the epidural, I was fully dilated and ready to push. No longer wracked with hurt and having released all of the pent-up emotions, I was able to focus all my energy on the pushing. After about another hour, I held my beautiful, healthy daughter for the very first time. As I looked into her swollen newborn face, elation, pride, and overwhelming love washed over me as all of the pain, all of the chaos, and all of the negative feelings that had fueled my meltdown simply faded away.

I didn't know it then, but that meltdown in the delivery room was the first of many yet to come. Since then, I've given birth to two additional daughters. Since then, I've had my fair share of meltdowns, some of them big and some of them small. I've yelled when I was angry because my children weren't following directions. I've felt an astounding sense of protectiveness when my child was being bullied. I've wept when I was frustrated as I listened to one of my babies "cry it out" just like the pediatrician recommended. I've panicked when I turned around and couldn't find my daughter at the zoo. I've pinched back tears and put on a brave smile when I dropped my daughter off for her first experience of being away from home for multiple nights in a distant city. I've also fought the incredible urge to run back and scoop her up when I got a call that she had been *briefly* separated from her group. I've been exhausted from caring for sick children and nights of very little sleep. I've lamented the last of the "firsts" as my youngest grows up.

My three daughters haven't even reached the teenage years yet, so I am certain there are more meltdowns to come. They will have their hearts broken and mine will break, too. They will get their driver's licenses, and I will pray for their safety as I watch them drive away alone for the very first time. They will go to college. They will get married. They will have their own families someday. When they do each of these things, I will cry tears of joy and fear and sadness and pride. Yes, there are many more meltdowns in my future.

Looking back, though, that first meltdown in the delivery room when I was barely even a mother taught me a very important lesson about motherhood. Despite my best efforts, motherhood simply will not always happen according to my plans. Sometimes plans are minimally altered such as when babies arrive a little late (or a little early) or when children catch the stomach bug or when soccer games get cancelled. Other times the changes are significant, such as when a job change requires moving to a different state or when pets pass away or when finances get tight. The fact is that things will inevitably go awry from time to time. When they do, I might get angry or sad or scared. I might meltdown again. And again. I can look back, however, and know that, even though meltdowns are unavoidable, they usually don't last long. Most of the time, there is a happier ending waiting on the other side of the meltdown, too.

If things aren't going according to *your* plans and you feel a meltdown coming on, go ahead and cry or scream or run away and hide. Then, lean on your support system, whatever or whoever it is; dust yourself off; regroup; try again; move forward. We're moms, and that's what we do—time and time again. The happy, the sad, the chaos, the meltdowns; they're all just a part of this beautiful journey.

Lisa Witherspoon is a stay-at-home mom and the Director of Household Operations in the "Spoon" household. She's been married to her traveling salesman husband for almost fifteen years and they have three daughters. Most of the time, you can find Lisa in front of her computer writing and trying to keep up with social media, using her minivan as a taxi to get her daughters to various events and practices, trying out a new recipe that her family will most likely not eat, or saying "yes" to yet another volunteer request. Lisa writes about her joys, frustrations, and memories on her blog, The Golden Spoons.

Why I Should Have Been Banned from the Doctor's Office

By Danielle Herzog
Martinis and Minivans

My period was three days late. This was the first month my husband and I were trying to get pregnant and people had warned us that it can take months when you first get off the pill. So when the picture on the stick showed a positive sign, I did what every freaked-out girl does. I took out the second, third, and fourth test, and I took them all at the same time. Then, I did something that most freaked-out girls don't do. I drove directly to the OB/GYN's office.

Yes, I drove right there without even an appointment. I walked up to the receptionist and said, "Um, I'd like a blood test because these say positive and there's no way that can be right."

Then, I did the grossest thing you can imagine. I dropped my pee sticks on her desk. Yep, dropped them right there for her to see. Yes, the caps were on them, but I'm not sure that really makes it less gross. She stayed very calm, looked down at the sticks and said, "You're pregnant. Now would you please remove those from my desk?"

I sheepishly picked up the sticks as she started using the antibiotic wipes next to her to clean her work area. I proceeded to go on and on to her about how there was no way I could be pregnant and that I desperately needed a blood test. People started staring, and I believe my arms were flinging so much that I looked like I was about to take off in flight. I might have also told the entire waiting room that I had just gotten off the pill after fifteen years on it and one date night should not have made me pregnant. Could a bottle of wine and some good sushi really have done this?

Thankfully, that incredibly patient receptionist called a nurse (probably more for protection against the insane girl who wouldn't leave her alone and flung pee sticks at innocent bystanders), and they quickly took me in the back to do a blood test.

While taking my blood the nurse said to me, "You know sweetie, you are probably pregnant so you are going to have to accept that fact."

No, no, no, why did they keep talking this nonsense? I mean, I knew I wanted to have a baby; but heck, I thought I would have a few months to get used to the idea. I thought that I would have some time to use fertilization calendars (not that I could ever understand them) or get tips from that crazy British nanny who solves everyone's parenting problems in just one hour.

When the blood test was finished, the receptionist told me to go buy something for the baby while I waited to hear from her. They would call me in about an hour.

That was the longest hour of my life. First, I went to get coffee. I knew if I was pregnant I shouldn't be drinking coffee and since I was determined to not be pregnant, I ordered a double espresso with a shot of chocolate. Then, I decided to do the inevitable and walk around a baby store. As I roamed the store, I would pick up an item then put it back. I repeated this process for over fifty-nine minutes. Finally, I just sat down on one of those nursing chairs in the furniture department and watched as babies cried and children pulled things off the racks. I watched in horror at what might be my future. All the moms looked frazzled and in need of a good haircut. I touched my hair that I spent forty minutes flat-ironing and decided I should just close my eyes instead.

As soon as the clock showed one hour passing, I jumped out of that ridiculously comfortable chair and called the OB/GYN office. The receptionist starting laughing when I told her my name. She simply said, "I told you so."

I then hung up the phone, closed my eyes, and cried. I probably sat in that chair for over ten minutes crying. However, when I lifted my hands from my face and took a deep breath, I realized I was crying tears of joy. Actual tears of joy.

And that is how I found out I was pregnant—bum-rushing a doctor's office, dropping my pee sticks on an innocent party's desk, and then looking like a shoplifter at a baby store. And you know what? I wouldn't change a thing. It was the best day of my life.

Danielle Herzog is the blogger behind Martinis and Minivans, a blog for anyone who has ever needed a martini after driving a minivan around all day. Or for anyone who has just ever needed a martini! A New Yorker now living the Midwest life as a somewhat sarcastic writer, mother, and wife, Danielle has been a freelance writer for over seven years. Her work has been featured on The Huffington Post, AOL.com, What to Expect.com, Scary Mommy, and Rants from Mommyland. She also writes a weekly parenting blog post and parenting advice column called "The Sassy Housewife" for the Omaha World Herald's site, Momaha. If it's part of her life, she'll write about it, except if it is about her mother—she promised her she wouldn't do that ...

Broken Glass

By Jennifer Kehl
My Skewed View

You don't know my son but, if you did, chances are you would be saying something like this, "How old is he? Seven? Really? And he just explained the second law of thermo-dynamics to me? I didn't even know there was a second law of thermo-dynamics."

And I would be sitting there nodding my head and saying, "Yep, I know. Uh huh. Yeah. It's crazy, isn't it? I don't know how he remembers this stuff." And finally, "Yeah, it's a blessing and a curse."

A blessing and a curse. A blessing AND a curse. A curse … a curse … a curse … echoes through my brain.

We call my son "The Deconstructionist" because he gets such pleasure from taking things apart. I encourage this behavior because I hope that someday the reverse will happen and he will decide to put something together—like an affordable personal robot or a flying car.

Take a stroll through my house, and you might find a dismantled cassette tape, the inside workings of a remote control car, or the pieces of a dryer strewn about the driveway.

Sometimes my son removes the pieces of his current "patient" with such expert care that I think, "Maybe he'll be a surgeon." After all, he can painstakingly locate just the perfect tools—the right-sized screwdriver or precision needle-nosed pliers. And I am more than happy to answer such questions as, "Mom, where are the pinchy things you use to get hair off of your face?" if his tool quest allows me thirty minutes of uninterrupted bliss to prepare homemade mac and cheese.

Other days, The Deconstructionist is less careful, and I replace the surgeon career option with a future job as a demolitions expert instead. Those days he is asking, "Where is Dad's hammer? My hammer has a short handle and I can't hit hard enough." It's on those days that I relegate him to the outside to do his banging and his deconstructing and his reverse inventing. I have learned to tune out the ridiculously loud noises that he can create on our back patio by turning up the music and focusing on another task. This turns out to be a blessing and a curse also.

When our dryer died and a new one arrived, The Deconstructionist asked if he could "take it apart before we threw it away." I figured, *What's the big deal? It doesn't work, it won't work, and in the end, some scrap metal guy is going to pick it up off the side of the road.* So we put the dryer on the patio and let him have his way with it.

Maybe I should have been more concerned when he came in to get his tool box. Maybe I should have cared when he went downstairs to retrieve his father's hammer. Maybe I should have heeded the red flashing warning lights when he asked me where his safety goggles were.

At first it was quiet as he worked his magic surgeon hands, carefully using his screwdrivers, wrenches, and assorted other tools that I myself cannot name. I peeked outside and saw various parts of the dryer on the ground and smiled quietly to myself thinking, *Surely he will learn something valuable from this and maybe he will even create the first … something.* I went back to my writing, cleaning, answering email, and cooking, knowing that he would probably stay busy for an hour, at least.

Then the banging started. I don't know if it was frustration or excitement. *Was there a plan to get to some internal target or was he just destroying?* But as I looked outside and saw him with the

hammer to the back of the dryer, it seemed my cue to turn up the music and maybe even vacuum.

And so I did. I vacuumed. I vacuumed the bedrooms, the playroom, the whole house. I vacuumed the heck out of the house, all the while jamming to my favorite disco tunes on my little iPod docking station in the kitchen, the room directly adjacent to the patio door. The room where, if I had looked out of one of the five windows, my heart would have stopped for a minute, and I would have had the wherewithal to stop the senseless destruction that was occurring right under my nose.

It is my bad, it really is. I know that once my son gets going with that hammer, the shear maniacal joy he feels sometimes overflows into an irresistible, uncontrollable urge to keep banging, and all his sensibilities leave him. And when the banging became more rhythmic, I should have realized that there was no longer a method to his madness—he was just destroying. But I did not.

And so, when I finished vacuuming and sneaked a look out the window, my cartoon eyes popped out as exclamation points circled my head. My son had smashed the glass front door of the dryer into itty bitty pieces all over the brick patio and flower beds, and he was busily crushing the bigger pieces into even smaller parcels of square-tempered glass.

Sheer panic took over as I ran out of the patio door screaming at the top of my lungs, "STOP! STOP! STOP!" His frenzy was in full swing, and he was actually laughing as he swung again and again, sending smithereens of tempered glass all over the yard. I yelled my son's whole name, "First Middle Last, STOP!" and got as close as I dared.

He looked at me, "What?"

"You are getting pieces of glass all over the yard!" My voice was now set to permanent screeching harpy. We then proceeded to have one of those parent-child conversations that make you want to take a hammer to your own head.

"Oh, but you said I could play with this. You said it was mine."

"Yes, I said you could play with it, but I didn't think you would break the glass."

"Well, I didn't know it was glass, at first. I thought it was plastic."

"But when you realized it was glass, why didn't you stop?"

"Well, it was fun."

At this point, my voice could have shattered the glass if any had remained. "It was fun? It was fun?! How much fun do you think it will be to clean it all up?!"

"Oh, but I can't clean it up," he said seriously.

"You sure can clean it up. You will help me clean it up right now."

"You said I'm not allowed to touch broken glass. You say that whenever a glass breaks. You say get out of the room until I clean up all the glass. So now you can clean up all the glass."

"What?! What did you say to me? I can clean up all the glass?! Dude, you will be cleaning up all of this glass this minute. Go inside and get your work gloves, which by the way you should have been wearing when you had this brilliant idea, and then you can help me pick up this glass."

And then The Deconstructionist simply said, "No."

"No? No? Who do you think you are? YOU did this, not me. This is YOUR responsibility, and I expect you to help me deal with this. Do you realize that the glass is everywhere? We won't be able to let the dogs outside until we find every single piece of glass, or the next thing you know we'll be at the dog emergency room."

He stared blankly at me.

"Go get your gloves." I marched to the side door to get the dustpan and broom. He strolled in the patio door to get his gloves. After cleaning for about ten minutes, I realized that he had not joined in the efforts yet. I went to the side door to call him but it was locked. Hmm. I must have locked it by habit when I came out with the broom. I went to the patio door and it was locked too. Crap. That door does not lock itself. I started pounding on

the door, screaming my son's name. I was screaming and yelling and pounding. The dogs were barking like crazy and jumping on the door and getting whipped into a frenzy, just as I was.

Then all of the sudden I stopped to listen. I noticed that the more the dogs barked, the more I heard another sound. The sound of a television getting louder and louder. The sound of a television drowning out the sound, my sound, the screeching harpy at the back door.

I started to pound on the windows of the TV room, but he couldn't see me through the window coverings. I was seething as I frantically started searching for the hidden key that I knew wasn't there because I had used it one other time when I accidentally habitually locked the side door.

This is where I just don't get kids. Did he really think that the madder I got, and the more he ignored me, the better it would be for him? Did he really think that I would stay outside the house forever?

Luckily, at that moment, my husband pulled up.

"What are you doing?"

"Looking for the key." My voice was hoarse from screaming.

"Are you getting sick? Where is the boy? How did you guys get locked out?"

"WE did not get locked out. YOUR SON locked me out."

"What? Why would he do that?" He pointed behind me. "Who let him do that?"

"Really? Who? Is there someone else here? Of course it was me, but I didn't think he would smash the glass."

"Well, why did you let him have the hammer?"

"I didn't *let him* have the hammer. He has a hammer, and we said he could have the dryer."

"Well, you should have known this would happen."

"I should have known? I should have known? So now this is my fault? The boy smashed glass all over the yard, the dogs are going to cut their feet open when they have to go outside to the bathroom, and he locked me out, and this is my fault?!" My voice was now raised to the point of hysteria. "You know what? If you and your son want to ever eat again, or ever see me again, you are going to deal with this."

"What? Why me?"

"Because if I have to clean this, we will all be on the ten o'clock news. So unlock that door, give me the car keys, and clean the freakin' backyard."

Then I grabbed the keys and my bag and flew down that driveway.

When I came back later, feeling guilty because I'm a mother and my husband doesn't know how to cook and my son would surely be starving, I found my husband vacuuming up the last of the glass. I couldn't even care that he was using the inside vacuum. I wanted to say, "Really? You think that's a good idea?" But I certainly wasn't going to look a gift horse in the mouth, and so I went inside.

The boy had the good sense to look ashamed and tell me he was sorry. I shook my head. He said it again and hugged me.

"Okay, baby, I know. But you know how naughty that was, right? You locked me out of the house. Forget that you broke all of that glass and you wouldn't help clean it up. You locked me out."

And then he started crying. At some point, when he comes down from his frenzies, the full weight of what he has done hits him, and he feels true remorse. It couldn't have worked better if he had orchestrated it, because now my heart melted. I hugged him close and said, "It's okay."

And I didn't have to clean up the broken glass.

Jen Kehl is a mom, writer, homeschooler, maven of music, self-proclaimed sensory processing disorder expert, food allergy pro, photographer, controller of chaos, John Cusack aficionado, and all-around interesting person who refuses to put herself into any one category (because that's boring). She shares what is important to her in the blog, My Skewed View.

You're at the Happiest Place on Earth. Why are You Crying?

By Dana Hemelt
Kiss My List

*D*isney World. Amazing how just two words can light up a child's face and turn the most calm and collected parent into a raving lunatic.

I happen to love Disney World, as do my husband and kids. We descended on the parks for the first time when my daughter, Gwen, was five and her brother, James, was two. They were delighted to embrace each character they encountered, each shyly extending their autograph book to fill it with signatures from Aladdin to Winnie the Pooh and everyone in between. James still napped in the afternoons, so we folded up the double stroller for a few hours each day to rest and decompress. It was a magical vacation, or at least that is how I choose to remember it.

Our encore visit occurred two years later, when the kids were seven and four. We had driven to Orlando the last time, but for this trip we boarded a plane for the kids' very first flight. Gone was the gargantuan double stroller, replaced by one flimsy umbrella stroller and Daddy's shoulders. The jackets, snacks, water bottles, and camera that were shoved in the bowels of the Graco double wide were now lugged around on Mommy's and Daddy's backs. Nap time was a thing of the past, as both children insisted they were big enough to stay in the parks all day. Tiny bladders, and no more diapers, meant hourly trips to the restrooms. Varying height requirements on attractions meant waiting around as we traded-off riders.

But we were in Disney World, and that makes up for those minor inconveniences. The smiles on my babies' faces as they hugged Goofy made me deliriously happy, and their screams and giggles as they rode Thunder Mountain Railroad were music to my ears. I indulged James's plea for an eight-dollar tattoo that came off hours later when his sister slathered sunscreen on his arm. To be fair, I allowed Gwen to get a hair wrap that survived through two months of hair washings until it mercifully slipped off one night while she was sleeping. We had dessert every night. We bought souvenirs that would be tossed in the back of the closet when we returned home. We watched every parade and stayed until nine o'clock one night to watch the fireworks.

Epcot is typically the least favorite park for kids, but mine loved it. After a day at Magic Kingdom and a good night's sleep, we headed to Epcot, bypassing Future World and going right to the World Showcase. We circled the countries, eating our way through each one. As we finished riding the Norway Maelstrom for the second or third time, we started walking towards the silver orb that is Spaceship Earth—the quintessential symbol of Epcot.

Holding my hand, Gwen begins to whimper and whine. I don't even remember exactly why. She is tired, but she refuses a ride on Daddy's shoulders or the stroller. She's hungry, but she refuses a snack from the backpack. She doesn't want to go to Spaceship Earth; she doesn't think she will like it even though she has no recollection of the ride from the first visit. Her voice is getting louder and louder, and her whining is reaching an uncomfortably high pitch. She stomps her feet and comes to a standstill. She crosses her arms in front of her chest and cocks one little hip to the side.

And then she says it—the most ridiculous, incongruous statement I had ever heard come out of her mouth.

"THIS IS THE WORST DAY EVER!"

Are you kidding me?

I turn to my firstborn, thinking that I must have misheard her. Her whining must have reached a frequency that only dogs can hear; surely she did not say that this day in Disney World was the worst of the over 2,500 she had lived? That day she endured three shots at the pediatrician. Better than today? That day she stepped on the fin of that plastic toy dolphin, and it sliced her foot open. Rainbows and unicorns compared to today? I glance at my husband, who knows exactly where this is going. With our mental telepathy that had been honed to perfection after over seven years of co-parenting, he lets me know that I'm taking point for this battle.

I return my evil stare to Gwen, who now has chubby tears rolling down her face and dropping onto her Disney Princess cardigan. Never one to back down, she meets my gaze and starts in with the "I don't wanna's." Every parent knows them; they signal the point of no return. Gwen will say "I don't wanna" to anything I say, and this dam is going to burst.

My vision narrows and the world becomes the six-square-foot area that Gwen and I are occupying on the path between the World Showcase and Spaceship Earth. I know there are other people walking by, families with appreciative children and parents who aren't about to lose it. But I don't see them. I see only my precious, beloved daughter who is destroying this magical vacation.

What happens next is a blur. I begin talking to Gwen through gritted teeth, explaining how we have to be flexible and go with the flow. When this doesn't work, I abandon the reason and logic angle and opt for berating and guilt. I progress to medium-volume yelling, telling Gwen how ungrateful she is and how hard Daddy has worked to pay for this trip and how many children just dream about visiting Mickey Mouse and how it's the happiest place on Earth and HOW COULD YOU POSSIBLY BE CRYING IN DISNEY WORLD?!

My yelling is feeding her tears, and Gwen's tears are fueling my meltdown. My vision widens and I see the normal families strolling by and gaping at the crazy lady screaming at her poor, innocent kid. The moms avert their eyes and the dads shake their heads. The well-behaved kids stare like we are the newest attraction in the park. "Look, Mommy! No lines for this character signing! Can I get the Evil Queen's autograph for my book?"

My husband wisely decides that it's time for me to tag out, and he takes over with a calmer head. I sit down on a bench and take James's hand, wondering when he will turn on me. He smiles at me as he sees that the mommy he loves has reclaimed her body from Meltdown Mommy. My heart rate normalizes and I stop sweating profusely. By the time I am calm enough to once again lay eyes on my daughter, I look up to see Gwen and her daddy clasp hands and begin the walk to Spaceship Earth. I don't know how he tamed the beast, and I don't care. It was over, and I had not been taken away in handcuffs for creating a scene in the place where magic lives.

We have been back to Disney three times since that vacation, with fewer meltdowns each time and never one as huge. There have been other worst days ever, and I've learned to take them in stride and write them off as a strong-willed girl's melodrama. I've learned that ignoring them or staying calm makes them blow over faster, but it's hard for me to do that. After all, where do you think Gwen gets her stubbornness and quick temper?

On a subsequent visit to Epcot, the four of us were strolling down that same path after a lovely afternoon of visiting countries in the World Showcase. My husband and I were sipping beers from Germany, and the kids were munching on soft pretzels and comparing the pins they had traded with cast members. As we headed towards our ride on Spaceship Earth, we walked by a young family in the throes of a Mickey meltdown. A kid was crying, a mom was yelling, and dad and brother looked miserable and uncomfortable. I squeezed my husband's hand, smiling just

the tiniest bit, and passed my Evil Queen crown on to the next mommy having a meltdown.

———————

Dana Hemelt is using her Master's degree in Clinical Psychology to stay at home and raise two brilliant, well-adjusted children. Never without a project, Dana started her blog, Kiss My List, as a way to channel her slightly obsessive energy. She's the next great novelist, stand-up comic, fashionista, and interior decorator all trapped in the body and life of a suburban mom. At least that's how she's sees it in her head.

From Goldilocks to Dreaded Locks

By AnnMarie Gubenko
Tidbits from the Queen of Chaos

I could write about the meltdown I had when my oldest son, Nico, then ten, jumped down a flight of stairs to see what would happen and ended up on crutches. I could write about the time when Tommy and Isabella were two, and they ate a box of Pepto-Bismol tablets thinking it was pink candy and had to be rushed to the ER. I could write about the time that Belle stuck an M&M up her nose and couldn't get it out and we ended up, yep, in the ER. Or I could tell you about the time when Belle accidentally pushed Gia and split her lip which resulted in … wait … yes … the ER. But ER visits are meltdowns that are a dime a dozen in our house.

Some would say it's a rite of passage. I would say it was the cause of a major meltdown by what should have been a mature, 35-year-old.

There I was folding laundry when my little blondie, Belle, came up to chat. She was named for the princess because we thought surely with my dark-haired genes she'd look like her. Instead she looked more like Tinker Bell. She was four and it was the beginning of October. We were talking about which Wiggle was the cutest, when I noticed my lovely daughter's eyes were popping a bit more than usual. Looking closer, I saw her normal, blond lashes looked awfully dark, almost black.

"Belle, do you … do you have make-up on? Were you playing in my make-up?" I asked her.

She looked at me innocently and said, "Nooo."

I squinted to see her better and saw that her face was flushed, an immediate sign she was lying.

"Belle, I see your Mommy Dot. I *know* you have make-up on." She began to cry at having been caught in a lie. When Nico was little, I used to tell him that if he ever lied, a dot would appear on his forehead that only I could see; hence the name, Mommy Dot.

"No, I don't. The Mommy Dot is wrong."

As she cried those words and the tears fell, two black streaks formed on her face.

"Sweetie, look in the mirror." She was busted and I was livid, not because she played with my make-up but because she had lied. I have zero tolerance for lying. She began to sob that she was sorry. I sent her to her room and told her to think about what she had done. Usually she would call out every five minutes, "Can I come out?" This time I didn't hear a peep out of her. I should have guessed then that she was up to something since a quiet child is usually a naughty child. I thought maybe she had fallen asleep, and a sleeping four-year-old should never be disturbed.

I was really busy with the other two kids and when she called to come out, I just yelled that it was fine. I remember making dinner (in the days before travel sports when I actually still made dinner) and telling her I was upset that she played in my make-up when she knew she wasn't allowed to. I explained that she was sent to her room because she had lied about doing it and that under no circumstances was she to lie to me ever again. Growing up, my parents would often put the fear of God in my sisters and me, since it always kept us from lying or misbehaving. I might have thrown in that lying was a sin and that it made God mad, too, for good measure. He doesn't even have to see the Mommy Dot. He just knows.

The rest of the night was relatively normal: refereeing a few fights, reprimanding Nico for staring at Belle in a funny way, which caused her to scream at a pitch that I am sure made dogs' ears bleed, and grabbing Tommy before he jumped off the top of a dresser. Bath time couldn't have come soon enough. As I was washing Belle's hair, something seemed strange but I couldn't put my finger on it. As I was combing her wet hair, I pulled the comb through her bangs and again, something didn't seem right. Then it hit me.

She had no bangs! The whole middle section of her bangs was *gone!*

Belle had the most beautiful hair. It was long, blond, and soft. She had cascading curls with full bangs. It was the hair I had always wanted—hair that she would let me put up in different styles constantly. People were always telling her how pretty her hair was. Once a woman had told me that Belle's hair looked like "an angel itself kissed her." Now all that was left of the front of her hair was a jagged tuft. To say I handled myself well would be a complete and utter lie. I believe what actually happened was this …

"Oh my God, Belle! What did you *do*?" I yelled.

She immediately started crying.

"What *did* you *do*?" I yelled. If you could imagine a wide-eyed, crazed person grabbing her darling daughter's head and searching and willing the hair to be there, you would have had me at that very moment.

Belle cried some more and offered muffled apologies.

"What the *hell* did you do? Where is your hair? Did you *cut* your hair? Did you *freaking* cut your hair? Where did you get scissors?"

Belle cried some more. "In my room," she sniffed.

"You have pictures this week, and your beautiful hair is gone!"

"I'm sorry, Mommy."

I realized that she was just as upset as I was, and I pulled her onto my lap. She looked at me with her big, green eyes and looked so pathetic with the missing hair that I said, "It's okay. We'll fix it." I then burst into tears and dialed my friend, neighbor, and hair dresser, Jen. I'm not sure I even spoke English when she answered.

"Jen, oh my God, Belle cut her bangs off. Not just a snip—completely off. All the way to her scalp. She has pictures this week, and I don't think there is anything anyone can do to fix it. It's jagged and, Jen, there is no hair there. None, and now we are going to have this moment memorialized forever with her four year old preschool picture. I can't believe she cut her hair off! What do I do?" I huffed out of breath.

Jen told me that it was her experience that this was a rite of passage for little girls. *It was?* Growing up, I had a bowl haircut and longed for long hair that I could put up in ponytails. I wouldn't have dared to cut my hair on purpose. Plus, I'm not even sure my mother let me hold scissors until I was old enough to know not to cut anything but paper. I think cutting was my only "needs improvement" grade in all my years in school.

Jen had us walk over and she calmed us both down. She had a way about her that immediately made you feel like it was going to be okay. When my stylist before her made me look like Eddie Munster, with a bad dye job, Jen calmly said, "We'll just fix this right up," and she did. I think on that particular night with the size of the meltdown I was having, it took a margarita to finally stop glaring, yelling, and crying.

So while Jen calmly took care of the jagged patch of hair, I wondered if hats for four-year-old pictures would look good or if maybe berets were in style. *Why couldn't this have happened around Easter?* Target always had cute Easter hats. I thought about the possibility of her wearing a headband, but that meant I'd have to buy her a new dress which meant she would also need new shoes. It was turning into an expensive "rite of passage." Then I switched gears and thought about how Belle was destined to be as scissor-challenged as I was, because it was going to be a very long time before I let her near a pair of scissors again.

Jen was a miracle worker, and to everyone else, Belle looked like she had bangs. Even today, when I look at that school picture, I can see where she cut it. In a way, my meltdown was justified. Her hair never did grow back normally, so she had to grow out her bangs to cover the cowlick she gave herself. Since the "incident" she has always worn her hair down to the middle of her back and I still cringe when anyone takes scissors to it.

Much to my dismay and as soon as she was old enough to do her own hair, her Goldilocks' curls were gone. She never had the appreciation for her natural curls and preferred wearing her hair straight. The irony of the whole experience is that Belle recently told me that she wanted to be a hair stylist when she gets older. She said she wanted to only style hair, not cut it. I wonder if that's because the last time she cut any hair, the reaction was a total meltdown.

This story comes up from time to time and Belle always describes it as the "time Mom totally freaked out." It was not one of my proudest moments as a mom especially when it was all over and I realized that I'd had a complete meltdown over hair.

AnnMarie Gubenko is a former teacher, aspiring writer, and stay-at-home mom of four here on earth and one in Heaven. She married her college sweetheart, and together they are riding this roller coaster of life. When not shuffling kids to football, basketball, baseball, cheerleading, volleyball, and ballet, and folding and putting away the endless mounds of laundry that a family of six creates, she loves to read, write, and can often be found at Target or Barnes and Noble. She is the author of Tidbits from the Queen of Chaos, a blog about the ups and downs of marriage to a sports-loving extrovert and motherhood involving a teen, twins, and a preschooler. Topics such as infertility, life with children that battle chronic illnesses, and triumphing through tragedy are also covered. It's not always pretty, but it's always honest.

BONUS #1

The Dirty Dozen: Coping with a Mommy Meltdown

By Melissa Swedoski

Mom #1: "This one time I had a meltdown right in front of my in-laws. I said seven different cuss words and then stormed out of the room. Now they're afraid to come back to our house."

Mom #2: "That's nothing. This one time I had a meltdown in the school parking lot, and several parents and a couple of teachers heard me cussing like a sailor on leave at the bar. Thank goodness school security was already clocked out for the day."

Mom #3: "I can beat that. This one time I had a meltdown at the park. Cops were called. The ambulance arrived. I may have blacked out and lost a few days' memory while at the hospital. But I'm much better now."

If you've had a child, you've been there, at least once. The moment when your nerves are frayed, your humor is gone, your body is shaking, and all you can find the strength to do is yell. A lot.

Mommy meltdowns can run from a mild, fist-clenching moment, all the way to epic, crying, screaming, hair pulling (yours, not theirs), only-seen-on-reality-TV moments. Thankfully, there are ways to cope. And not all of them involve alcohol.

Here's a dirty dozen to consider. And just like any dozen, keep what works and throw out the rest. Make sure you bag them, and put them on the curb so they don't start to smell.

Use your parenting partner in crime. As a punching bag if necessary. If it's your husband, you may want to drop kick him in the pants, but try to avoid this, since you will probably want to use those parts at a later date.

Drink. Doesn't have to be wine or liquor. In fact, it's best to avoid those before 10:00 a.m. A cool glass of water—splashed in your face if you have to—can do the trick, or a quick taste of that awesome homemade lemonade that you were saving for your kids to use for their roadside stand might be enough to put you back in balance.

Make a call. Best to avoid calling 911 to complain about your emotional meltdown, unless you've been longing to meet members of your local emergency response team in uniform. But you can call one of your mom friends or your own mom or sister or aunt. Or text or email, so they can have something to do during their lunch break.

Figure out how to turn on the funny and learn to laugh. Loudly and frequently. Kids know when they are pushing your buttons. Even if they don't, they figure out pretty quickly what's going to drive you crazy. So turn the tables and just start laughing at their behavior. Tell them how silly they are, so the moment turns into a memory that you can all share for years to come at the Thanksgiving dinner table. And then laugh at yourself, because once you consider it, that raving lunatic you were a few minutes ago most likely looked pretty silly.

Embrace the crazy. If you keep it all bottled up, you're only going to be worse for wear over the long run. It's real and it's hard, but it's the most in-the-moment you may ever be. And if you're lucky, someone's catching it all on video for you.

Leave the scene. This doesn't mean you can leave your child at the grocery store, library, restaurant, tire store, gas station, or clothing establishment. But you can put everyone in the car and drive off, or take everyone to the park. If you're at home, set the kids loose in the backyard so you can think and they can run. It will change the mood of the moment almost instantly.

Remind yourself, "You lived another day. They lived another day. It is a good day." You might want to embroider it on a pillow so you have something to muffle your screams when it happens again. Feel free to develop your own mantra for use in times of crisis.

Exercise. If they're small, put the kids in the stroller and take them for a walk or jog. If they're bigger, let them loose while you run the length of the yard or around the house or around the apartment complex. Turn on a music channel and just dance yourself silly. No room for all that bustling? Try deep breathing exercises and go into a deep meditative state where you can't hear anyone. If it works for Buddhist monks, why can't it work for you?

Check the effect. Is anyone's behavior improving since you unleashed the meltdown? Did the kids stop fighting? Did they run away and hide? Are you now alone with the rest of the cookies? Consider it a win.

Make time for you and help head off some of those meltdown moments. Be kind to yourself, and that doesn't mean squeezing in an extra thirty minutes of social media time. Take a bath or shower, sneak a nap, read a book, do your nails, watch some trashy TV, but above all, make sure it's something you like to do that seems like a real treat.

Put yourself in time out. Everyone is human and everyone has a bad day. Might as well let the kids know that it can happen to adults, too. You can let them know you need a moment and lock the bathroom door, or you can sit in your dark, cool closet. Just make sure to remove yourself from timeout before you fall asleep in the corner and the kids have a chance to take over the house.

Tell the truth. Don't try to deny your feelings or pretend like it didn't happen. When you invalidate yourself, you only feel worse in the long run. You're not alone, and there are plenty of mom bloggers out there who can testify to that. Write it down for yourself, and then you can publish it, throw it away, or keep it as a reminder for the next time.

The greatest motherhood truth is to recognize that you are not alone. Someone, somewhere has felt the way you do. She has had to pick herself up off the floor and keep moving forward. She has had to pick up shattered pieces of glass or ceramic from something flung in anger. She has had to apologize, and she is still here, working toward that elusive Mother of the Year award.

Slow Burn

By Alexa B.
No Holding Back

In some ways, my entire third pregnancy could be classified as one slow-burning meltdown.

It didn't get off to a very good start. I had just left the work force to stay home with my three-year-old and fifteen-month-old. I thought that staying at home with my two little ones would be a cake walk. There was no way it could be harder than working with a bunch of egotistical males in the law enforcement community. After all, most of my colleagues behaved like children on a daily basis. I could handle this.

Boy, was I in for a surprise!

On the first day I woke up ready to start this wonderful world of full-time mommy, only to realize that I had *no idea* what to do with two small children all day. My world had always been to pick them up, feed them dinner, bathe them, play with them, read together, and put them to bed. I had that routine down pat. The weekends were family time. Now I realized I had to keep them entertained *all day!*

So, I did what all good moms do—I turned on PBS Kids and called the woman who had been keeping them while I was working to find out what their schedule usually was.

We read some books, ate a snack, and watched some kids' shows. *Now what?* It was only mid-morning, and I was out of ideas. I really had no desire to read any more books or to sit on the floor and play with Bob the Builder toys.

Later, my neighbor invited me to try the local Mom's Club. She said it would help me by providing get-togethers and outings for the kids, and I would have some adult support. The next event was a park play date, so I decided to give it a try. FAIL.

Unfortunately, my first full week as a stay-at-home mom was spring break. That meant that the moms came to the park in force and brought all of their children. The older boys found their fun in teasing the younger ones, taking away their toys and chasing them around the playground. My three-year-old son spent most of the time screaming and crying because the big boys kept taking away his toys and tormenting him.

The fifteen-month-old spent her time running all over the playground. She would find ways to climb up into places that made me nervous, and I tried to keep up with her. There was no time for chatting with the other mothers or relaxing. *Where was the motherly support and sipping cups of coffee over conversation while our children played together?* While consoling my son for the fiftieth time, I looked up to find my daughter standing on the edge of a platform that was much too high for a toddler. As I darted over to get her, I did not look up before climbing to the platform and banged my forehead on the metal monkey bars. Ouch. Mega ouch.

Tears welled up in my eyes, partly from pain, partly from frustration, but mostly from fear that I had made the wrong choice in leaving my career. I was not good at this full-time mommy thing. I felt lonely and sorry for myself. I felt like a bad mother. I just wanted to scoop up my children and head to the comfort of my house.

But, oh no, there was one more encounter that stood in my way. As I tried to pull myself together, a little girl walked up to me and told me my baby girl was cute. Just as I was starting to relax and feel better, she pointed at my belly and asked, "Is there a baby in your belly?"

All the frustration and my own personal insecurities came rushing forward. "No, I'm just fat!" I snapped. That was enough for me for that playdate. I snatched my two unhappy toddlers and carried them off to the car. The Mom's Club and I were not a match made in heaven. Eventually I would begin to fit in with them, but that's a different story.

A month after the infamous park play date, as I was still struggling to find my way in my new role as full-time mommy, I became pregnant. With *twins*.

Panic set in. The slow burn to meltdown had begun.

I had gone to the doctor by myself for the first ultrasound, because this was our third pregnancy, and I didn't think my husband needed to be there for this particular appointment. They had scheduled me pretty early (not even seven weeks), but luckily, they were still able to find a heartbeat and verify that all was well.

Then the ultrasound technician said something weird.

"So when mothers come in this early for the first ultrasound, we like to have them come back two weeks later just to verify that there aren't two babies."

"Huh?" I was dumbfounded. "Do you *see* two or is this a normal process?"

"I see two heartbeats."

Shock. And. Awe.

This strange, low, almost maniacal laugh began to erupt from my body. I'd never heard myself laugh like this and, truthfully, I hoped I would never make that sound again. I just kept laughing like a madwoman at the thought of four children four years and under. Dear God in Heaven above.

I had only been a stay-at-home mom for just over a month. I still did not even know what to do with the two children that I had. And yet, I was absolutely in awe over the idea of carrying twins. As an adolescent, completely wrapped up in *Sweet Valley Twins* and later *Sweet Valley High* books, I thought it would be so cool to have twins. But I never believed it would happen.

The ultrasound technician had the other tech come in along with one of the doctors, who both verified two heartbeats and two sacs, but only one placenta.

I vaguely remember the doctor nonchalantly informing me that one placenta meant the babies were identical, and there was a risk that they may not share the placenta equally. But, if that happened, there were things they could do to fix it. I had no idea that what she was actually telling me was that there was a 20 percent chance the babies could become extremely sick and risk dying if they developed Twin to Twin Transfusion Syndrome (TTTS,) but that did not come into play until the week twenty anatomy scan.

I could not reach my husband for several hours to share the news, but when I did he was in such shock he hung up on me. Clearly he also needed a moment to process things. By the time he got home from work, he was giddy.

The next few weeks were miserable. I had two little ones who wanted my attention *all the time.* I was so nauseated all I could eat were crackers and sour candies. I wore Sea Bands. By fifteen weeks, I felt thirty weeks pregnant. My back hurt, I felt like my belly was enormous, and I could not stand for more than two minutes without being incredibly uncomfortable.

Also, I was beginning to get a strange feeling. At seventeen weeks into the pregnancy, we went to a twins' consignment sale. Something told me not to buy a lot of matching clothes. I even felt a little nervous about buying the matching crib sets.

And then the day arrived that changed my life—September 28, 2011. It was the day of our twenty-week anatomy scan. My husband picked me up. It was a beautiful, warm day. I remember noting how pretty the sky was as we drove to the hospital, talking about many different things. I was really excited for my husband to have the opportunity to see the girls interacting together in the womb. At some point I told him, "I just hope there are two healthy babies in there."

An hour later, we would find out the babies were dying. They had developed TTTS and it was severe. They were not sharing the placenta equally. One baby was receiving too much fluid and was showing signs of cardiac distress and excess fluids building up in her body. The other baby was measuring entirely too small for this gestational point.

After the ultrasound, we waited for the doctor in one of the rooms. She came in and told us that our babies had Twin to Twin Transfusion Syndrome, I was being admitted to Labor and Delivery (L&D), and my care was being transferred to a Maternal Fetal Manager or a high-risk OB.

I asked her if anything could be done to save them. I will never forget the look on her face as she shook her head no.

I began to cry. They put me in a wheelchair, and one of the nurses began to wheel me across the hospital to L&D. The whimpers became sobs. The sobs became something greater, almost to the point of howling. I did not care who saw me or who heard me. The poor nurse kept patting my shoulder and murmuring, "There, there." I even heard her gasp back a sob at one point, too. My husband did not make a sound. This was probably a good thing since I sounded like a banshee, howling all the way across the hospital. This level of emotion surprised me because up until a few weeks prior, I had been absolutely terrified about having twins with two other small children.

But now, at twenty weeks gestation, I *wanted* these babies. I wanted them so badly. And immediately I had a new understanding for the absolute devastating pain that is caused by losing a baby or babies early in a pregnancy. I could not imagine anything more painful.

We still did not know what was happening. Why were we going to L&D? Were the babies going to die that day? Were they going to induce labor? My OB had really told us nothing at all.

As the nurse wheeled me through the double doors, Brooke, an L&D nurse who I would come to know well over the next ten weeks, ran to meet us and quickly took me into a little room. I was instructed to undress and get on the bed, where they hooked me up to some monitors. It felt like we waited for*ever*. During this time I listened to a crazy lady in the next room begging the doctor for stronger medicines for her unending headache and the lady on the left explain to the nurse that she was so proud she had cut back to only one pack of cigarettes a day. I became *angry*. I had done everything I was supposed to do. *Why would this happen to us?*

Finally we were seen by one of the MFMs on call. She assured us that there *are* things that can be done to try to save the babies, and we would start by having a procedure called an amnio-reduction the next morning to remove some of the excess fluid in Baby A's sac.

I was admitted to the anti-natal ward, and my husband left to make arrangements for the children and get the items I would need for three days in the hospital.

The next morning we were seen by my new doctor. He assessed the babies and gave us a rather bleak outlook. Baby A was sicker than he thought. There was not only fluid in her abdomen, but also fluid around her heart. Baby B was so tiny. But my doctor was hopeful that reducing the fluid in Baby A's sac would help things balance back out.

For an hour they drew fluid out of my abdomen. It was uncomfortable, but I got to watch the entire process on the computer screen, which was amazing. I saw my baby trying to grab the needle tip. I saw her kicking her sister in the head. We saw them both moving around like happy babies. They certainly did not look like they were ready to die, and I was not ready to give up on them.

The next twelve hours would be crucial. This procedure could cause preterm labor, and if labor could not be stopped, there would be no saving them at this juncture. The doctor told me that my only goal for the next four weeks would be to stay pregnant. At twenty-four weeks, they might have a chance.

Thankfully, there were no preterm labor issues. I was released from the hospital with orders to see the doctor each week for progress checks.

We made it to twenty-four weeks, but then the babies took a turn for the worse. The fluid had built up so much in Baby A's belly that her abdomen measured the size of a thirty-two week-old baby. Baby B was still too tiny. She wasn't going to make it at that size.

We needed to have another reduction. This time fluid would also be drawn out of Baby A's belly. So I was admitted to the hospital again.

Since we were at the point of "viability," by a technical standpoint, the first night in the hospital would be to give me all of the help that they could to prepare the babies for preterm birth. Steroids for lung development. Extra fluids and oxygen for me. And then, the dreaded magnesium sulfate.

Magnesium sulfate is often given to try to delay preterm labor. The doctor explained to me that research has also shown it may reduce the likelihood of cerebral palsy in preterm babies as well. But the side effects are nasty. I mean *nasty*. It's safe to say that magnesium sulfate (and the stress of the situation) can be blamed for the meltdown that was progressing from slow burn to nuclear explosion.

I do not deal well with stress. I never have. This is ironic because I am very good at adding stress to my life. When I feel excessively stressed, I begin to feel like a rubber band about to snap at any moment. I feel like my head is doing the thing that evil zombies do in movies where their heads shake back and forth really fast. Not quite spinning all the way around, but just nodding "no" in turbo speed.

When I'm stressed, I lose my cool. I snap at people.

I rarely have a full on meltdown because I am too passive aggressive; but I can give you looks that melt steel. And I huff and puff enough to blow your house down.

It is unusual for me to break into a full-on, crying, yelling, crazy town fit. However, given the right circumstances, even passive aggressive people can experience a thermal meltdown.

There is one thing that I am even worse at handling than stress and that is physical pain. Combine the two elements together, and you create the perfect storm for the mother of all meltdowns, Alexa-style.

Enter the magnesium sulfate. It was given to me through an IV. It did not take long before my blood began to feel like it was on fire. My mouth got really, really dry, and I remember screaming at my husband to get me something cold to drink.

I kicked the sheets off. "Take my socks off!" I hollered at my husband. "I'm on FIRE!"

Then the nausea kicked in. "I'm gonna baaaaarrrrrffff!" I hollered. I was crying and yelling and miserable.

The nurse came in and got a puke bag. As she looked at me, she began to laugh. I saw nothing funny about the situation. "Why are you laughing at me?" I hollered.

"You look like Ren and Stimpy!" she laughed. I did not find that funny at all.

"I look like an ugly, bug-eyed dog?" I started crying again.

"No, that's not what I meant. You know how they get mad and get really red?"

I had a vague recollection of those stupid dogs getting all red and gross-looking.

"You're all red and sweaty, and it just reminded me of that," the nurse continued.

I wanted to jump out of the bed and punch her in the nose. "I just want this to be over!" I sobbed to my husband. "I don't even care about the outcome anymore. I just want to be done." Those were words I would later regret terribly. But at that moment, I was in such a state of discomfort and pain, stressed and scared. I did not want to be doing this.

My husband tried to comfort me.

My sister was also in the room and tried to remind me that this was short-term pain for a long-term benefit. At least that's what we hoped.

I'm pretty sure I may have hissed or growled at them, and I am sure the language choice was not very nice.

About that time my sister's phone beeped. She looked at the text and started laughing.

"What's so funny?" I yelled at her.

"It's a text from Gayle. She says 'Did they give Alexa magnesium sulfate? If so, watch out! That's what Stephanie was on, and she said it makes you crazy!'"

"Noted," I replied, and we couldn't help laughing. Thankfully the effects were beginning to wear off, but the shame was starting to set in!

Over the next six weeks, we would continue to do everything we could to save the babies. At twenty-six weeks, I was admitted on twenty-four hour monitoring until the babies were born. I wound up being on hospital bed rest for over a month, during which time we had many more amnio-reductions. Baby A's condition continued to worsen, while Baby B grew slowly. But I stayed optimistic. They were still alive.

At thirty weeks and five days gestation I went into labor on my own. My little girls were born. They were both born alive. Kathryn, the larger baby, was four pounds, five ounces, largely due to excess fluid. Baby B, "Tiny," weighed one pound, ten ounces. But we heard her cry at delivery.

They were whisked off to the NICU. For two days, Kathryn fought hard, but could not overcome the damage that had been done to her body. Her heart and lungs gave out, and we said goodbye after fifty-two hours.

Tiny spent eighty-four days in the NICU, and came home in March 2012. I am happy to report that she is a perfectly healthy, thriving little miracle.

Alexa B. is the mother of four beautiful children, three on earth and one in Heaven. She blogs as "Kat Biggie" at No Holding Back, which was started primarily as an outlet for her grief after the loss of one of her twins. Alexa's goal is to bring more awareness to Twin to Twin Transfusion Syndrome (TTTS) and provide hope to other grieving mothers. Her blog also chronicles her adventures as a stay-at-home mother. Alexa is a wife, mother, writer, advocate, and sometimes political activist.

Beginning With the End in Mind

By C. Lee Reed
Helicopter Mom and Just Plane Dad

My meltdown officially began the day my only daughter, Beloved, was born. She was a wonderfully unexpected surprise pregnancy (yes, they do happen), and Just Plane Dad and I had no idea what we were in for. Fast forward nine months and my world is completely turned upside down by this beautiful, blonde-haired and blue-eyed girl. It was our beginning.

My journey to raising this amazing creature has been like everyone else's: first smile, first word, first crawl, first step, first day of school, first best friend, and the unbearable first broken heart. Unfortunately, along the way, I never realized that all of these firsts would eventually lead to the last: the last time she was a kid, the last time she was a student, and the last time she lived at home.

Beloved took her time with most situations, except talking (she is my child after all), and I remember the pressure from other parents to coax her along. Like robots, I listened to the experienced parents and spent an inordinate amount of time coaxing my only child to grow up. It started innocently enough. A small nudge up onto her arms to help her crawl and then she did! Constructing pillow forts to keep her sitting up straight by herself and then she could! Steadying her little bottom as she lightly clung to the side of the couch and pulled herself up—success! Cajoling her with outstretched arms and a cookie for that ever important first step, which she finally took on her first birthday. Why oh why did I push so hard?

Even her physician was in on the ruse. "She's very petite for her age," she'd say. "Normally babies on breast milk gain weight quickly." So Just Plane Dad and I would pray that our baby was healthy and that she'd catch up to other children eventually. I fed her on demand and ensured that our home was filled with a variety of wholesome foods, lest she become a picky eater and not thrive. Happily, I accomplished the feat of raising an average-sized child. Yes, it took fourteen years, but it was time well spent.

The first day of school was the beginning of the crack in my heart that brought about my meltdown. My beautiful child had spent every day of her short life with her dad and me, safely at home under our watchful eyes. Nobody told me how difficult it was going to be seeing my daughter all dressed like a "grown-up" and heading off independently into her classroom.

Nobody explained how hard it is to leave your baby with a group of people she doesn't know and how hard you'll pray when leaving that she doesn't cry for you. *Why isn't this in parenting books?*

Moving to middle school brings about a whole new set of firsts. Creak, crunch, crack. Seemingly over the summer, all of the icky boys at school turn into handsome, little heart-stealing thieves. My daughter grew up with guy friends, so it never occurred to me or her father that these would turn romantic; or as romantic as can be expected in eighth grade. The first time I saw my daughter hug another boy that wasn't her father, my hands went numb! Did he just hug her back? Oh no, this can't be. But, alas, it was. Relationships have arrived and it's time for me to play catch-up. Somewhere over the summer break, my kid became a potential suitor for boys and I missed it. I can feel my heart palpitations starting already. And I dread seeing my little girl's face after Romeo has broken her heart. Thinking back to my own experiences, we just sort of dealt with the dating and break-up scene. But now that it's happening to my girl, I start

to relive those feelings and my heart weeps for her. "Yes, honey, you will get through this and find another boyfriend. Don't rush it though; you have all the time in the world." If only that were true.

Did you hear that crack? I heard it loud and clear. No worries, it's just me trying to keep it together.

Today is Beloved's first driving lesson with Mom. I find myself sitting in a car in the middle of a huge parking lot of our local grocer with my only daughter. The school did their part by teaching her the finer points of driving, and now it's my turn for the real-life application.

In her roughly-manicured little hand, she holds the key to her future. The ever-admired driving permit; her ticket to the impending driver's license. Thankfully, the permit means we are still at least one year away from the actual driver's license, but try explaining that to a teenager.

Her eyes light up and she proudly extends the small, glossy photo high above her head. I can already sense her Facebook account filling up with well-wishes and congratulatory notes from her tight-knit group of friends. The permit is a badge of honor and she intends to wear it well. For me, it's an ever-constant reminder that one day she will be eligible for her driver's license. And with the driver's license comes age; almost an adult that can make her own decisions. I quickly think back to me and her father pushing so hard for her to walk, and I wonder why we were so misguided? Why didn't those parents tell us that walking will lead to driving and then to leaving? Silently, I vow to tell all new moms I meet the truth about those lovely "firsts"—they suck! Crack, crack.

Which brings me to today. All of her other firsts have led me to this very moment. Beloved is excited and rightfully so. She tests for her driver's license today. I sit in a fuzzy stupor watching her primp and powder her nose. "I need my picture to be perfect," she says. I wonder to myself how it could be anything but. "I hope I don't crash into anything," she says. I nod in agreement.

The only crashing I can think about is my heart into my throat as the prospect of my daughter actually passing this test and driving on the road … alone … scares me. Did my mother feel this way? If she did, I never noticed. And to her credit, she never let me see if she felt like I do at this moment. It wouldn't have been fair. Just like it wouldn't be fair if I opened my mouth right now and said something stupid to my daughter. Beloved is on cloud nine and is already planning out her first trip in the car. I smile as I watch her scurry around tending to the most important thing today—her to-do list.

We hop in the car and head over to the vacant school parking lot for some last minute practice. She doesn't need it. It's simply my way of prolonging the inevitable. She humors me for about an hour and then reminds me that we need to be prompt for her test. Yes, we do; she's right.

We arrive and sign in, and she takes the picture that will adorn her license for the next five years. Five years. My baby will be twenty-one the next time she has to "say cheese" at the DMV. My mind starts racing over the last years of her life, and I keep hearing the voices of those that came before me. "Don't blink, it goes fast!" *Fast?* Fast is an understatement. Warp speed is not significant enough to describe what has just happened to my little girl. The doctor handed her to me at the hospital just a few days ago, *didn't she?* Didn't we just buy a dress for her middle school graduation? Sadly, no.

The instructor calls her name and Beloved stands up, now realizing the significance of this moment in time. She nervously bites her lip. Through tears, I wish her luck and kiss her forehead. "Do your best honey, you've got this," I say. She walks out the door, and I have to catch myself to keep from falling over. The stiff plastic chairs do nothing to comfort my pain. Please God, do not let her pass this test. And then, please God, she'll be heartbroken if she doesn't, so please guide her during the test. I sit and wait for the car to return.

Beloved's smiling face stares at me from across the room, and I know the truth. She now holds her future in her hands. This seemingly inconsequential piece of paper offers her the most coveted treasure of children her age—freedom. Freedom to drive herself to the mall, freedom to get a job that requires transportation, freedom to grab a movie with friends and, in the near future, freedom to leave her childhood home as she starts her own journey in life. Leaving is imminent.

She drives home excitedly talking about the tricky maneuvers on the test and how she aced them. She can't wait to tell Dad. He will be so proud! I nod and smile, trying to speak, but I've suddenly become mute. My body feels numb, and I hear the distant, ever-present cracking of my heart. My meltdown begins. My daughter has earned her driver's license. My breathing races. She is fast becoming an adult. My blood pressure increases and I start to sweat. I will no longer need to drive her places and will miss those special conversations that can only be held at red lights. Tears stream from my face, and I make no attempt at wiping them. I've earned every one. I am overwhelmed with joy for her new beginning and grief for the end of an era. I am broken. I am weary. I am sad. *Why did we rush this?*

C. Lee Reed, Helicopter Mom, along with Khris, Just Plane Dad, believe that you can stay highly involved in your children's lives and still maintain a happy, healthy, loving connection. Listen to their tales from the not-so Darkside of Parenting at their blog, Helicopter Mom and Just Plane Dad. Together they hope to change the world's perception of helicopter parenting by proving that no harm comes to children whose parents hover.

Excuse Me, Complete Stranger

By Debra Cole
Urban Moo Cow

I lost my cool on a fine January afternoon over one simple word: hat.

I live in New York, a city not known for its tact. Even so, I was unprepared for the lengths people would go to stick their nose into my pregnancy and parenting. The chatter accumulated until one day, a middle-aged man on the street said the word "hat," and I melted down.

By the middle of my third trimester, I'd had it with being pregnant. I had not slept horizontally in weeks. I waddled around sweating in November. Even my dog had given up sitting on my lap.

Still, I headed to Bath & Body Works to fulfill my filial stocking-stuffer purchasing duty. As I dragged my swollen body toward the door, the security guard stopped me specifically to inquire whether I was having twins.

At birth, my son was a slim five pounds, seven ounces. As uncomfortable as I might have felt, there was no way I was housing two babies. Unfortunately for this particular security guard, I had reached the limit of my patience with the endless, gratuitous commentary on my pregnant body.

"Nope," I chirped. "But thanks for calling me fat!"

I think he was genuinely confused.

Then, the week before I gave birth, I had an incident with our doorman, who looked and sounded like he had left the Bada Bing, stepped out of my television, changed out of his blindingly white track suit, and gone downstairs to make sure no one unauthorized entered the buildin'. Fuhgeddaboutit.

Apparently delighted by the newly installed video cameras in our laundry room, Bada Bing decided it would be entirely appropriate to comment, as I shuffled by, that he "would recognize those legs anywhere" and that I was so big he "could see the baby moving" on the screen. Seriously? *Seriously?*

Not surprisingly, we moved to Brooklyn five months later.

I thought once I gave birth, I would be done with commentary from the peanut gallery. I was wrong. Two months after our move, I ran into our new super in the elevator.

"Hi, how are you?" I asked.

"I'm fine, how are you?" he replied with a thick Dominican accent. Then he glanced at my mid-section and continued, "You are looking so much …" He trailed off, groping for the right word, and settled on "… *better*."

"Oh yeah, thanks," I said, trying to laugh it off. At least he wasn't scrutinizing the laundry videos for a glimpse of pregnant leg. "I guess I'm losing the baby weight."

"Aaaaah riiiiiight," he said, recalling my little cherub whom he had obviously forgotten. He wasn't making a comment about losing *baby* weight. Just *weight.* "The baby," he said. *That's why you were so fat.* The words hung unspoken in the air, suffocating us both. I couldn't wait to get off the elevator. Buh-bye.

C'mon, fellas. We know you are not trying to be rude. But give us a break. Just smile and say, "You look great." Take it from me. This is no time to get creative.

Living in Brooklyn with a little one can be difficult. To arrive at the "local" YMCA for baby swim class, I had two choices. I could take a subway two stops, which involved walking ten minutes to the train; carrying the stroller, my son, and our

twelve-pound bag filled with four days of rations—in case of, you know, Armageddon—down two flights of stairs; hoping someone offered me a seat on the train; carrying the stroller, my son, and our twelve-pound bag up two flights of stairs on the other side; and walking another ten minutes. Or, I could take a bus that was chronically late, snaked slowly through the public housing projects, and usually ended up having some kind of earring-pulling girl-fight on board.

Suffice it to say, I was always drenched in a layer of sweat and feeling defeated before I even arrived for splashy-splashy class.

One summer morning, minutes away from the entrance (I had chosen the subway), a middle-aged woman with a black T-shirt that said something like "Greedy People Suck" stopped to inform me that the inside of my stroller—which was covered with a thin, white, muslin blanket to keep the sun off—was probably up to 120 degrees by now. Since she was a nurse, she just wanted to let me know how many kids become dehydrated due to blanket-covered strollers and end up in the hospital where she works.

I am not really the nicest person around. My friends tell me I'm simply "direct," but I know my frenemies must use other choice adjectives. The brazenness of these random comments, however, had begun to stun me into an uncharacteristic silence.

I looked at her blankly, said thank you, and moved on. She obviously had not gotten the memo. We—and I speak for all mothers in the universe, past, present, and future—do not want your advice. Not even if you are a nurse. Or think greedy people suck. Do you know who sucks in that scenario? The one in which a mom has just traveled an hour to sing *Ring Around the Rosie* with strangers in an over-chlorinated yet inexplicably pee-filled indoor pool—wearing a *tankini*, no less—while the sweet fruit of her loin splashes cluelessly around for a half hour, and then you criticize her use of an overpriced receiving blanket? *You* do. Yes, you.

By winter, I had learned braving the subway was a whole hell of a lot easier if I strapped my son to my chest in the baby carrier and stashed him inside a special Papoose coat big enough to close around us both. Once bundled in, my son's round, hairless, disembodied head stuck out of the middle of the enormous puffy coat like a little Voldemort. Remember in the first Harry Potter movie where Professor Quirrell carried Voldemort in his turban? Yeah, like that.

Everyone raves about baby-wearing, but toddler-wearing is something else entirely. I have neither the shoulders nor the upper body strength to glide effortlessly along with twenty pounds strapped to my chest. I spent the entire winter swearing and perspiring from one place to another.

On my way to the subway in Manhattan one mild January afternoon, I called a friend who had been trying to conceive for months to see if she was free for lunch. She wasn't, but we chatted briefly about her recent doctor's appointment. Just then, I saw a fifty-something-year-old man walking toward me, gesticulating wildly with an appalled look on his face.

I narrowed my eyes in the silent but universally understood sign of *What? Is there a Tyrannosaurus behind me about to chomp my head off? Why else would you be interrupting my phone call, complete stranger?*

"Hat," he said, gesturing again, a bit more frantically as he passed. "Put a hat on the baby! It's cold out."

I. Almost. Lost. My. Mind.

It was the hat that broke the camel's back. I cracked under the invisible weight of comments and insults that had been heaped upon me, my body, and my mothering over the past two years.

"Really?" I said, turning to follow him down the street like a lunatic.

The man continued on his way, pretending to ignore me, which was ironic, considering I should have been the one to pretend to ignore *him*. But I did not. Oh, no, I did not.

"Really?" I continued, yelling. People stopped to stare at the woman carrying Voldemort who was verbally accosting an apparent stranger. Even by New York standards, I was acting a little crazy. "Is it cold out? I couldn't tell!" I called to him as I followed. "Do you think I should put a hat on him? I wasn't sure!"

Was I imagining things or was he picking up his pace a little so he could cross before the sign changed from the inviting white man to the forbidding red hand?

"Thanks for letting me know!" I screamed as he crossed the street.

I realized at that point that I had been holding the phone in my hand the whole time. My friend was still there, laughing. My heart was pounding; I was furious and not a little embarrassed.

What I should have said, I told her, was, "Excuse me, complete stranger, but did you carry this child in your uterus for nine months? No? Is that because he's not yours? Or because you don't even *have* a uterus of your own? Did you carry his twenty pounds strapped to your chest inside a parka made for the Arctic Circle from the ass-end of Brooklyn to the Flatiron District, sweating, late, and trying not to trip down the subway stairs and kill the both of you? Did you? DID? YOU? Are you me? ARE? YOU? No? Then, for the love of all that is holy, MIND YOUR OWN @$#%^* BUSINESS."

We humans are, frankly, a judgmental lot. We judge what someone is wearing or her choice of spouse; we swear we would never live in a particular city or paint our kitchen chartreuse. The difference is that, more often than not, we keep our collective trap shut. Why, then, is it open season on pregnancy and parenting?

Perhaps, deep down, we believe we should *already know how* to do this childrearing thing. Humans have been raising their young since the beginning of our species, for crying out loud. Shouldn't it be "natural" and "intuitive?" For all my education, shouldn't I be *at least* as competent in raising my child as, say, the first generation of Homo sapiens? Yet a cursory search will turn up book after nauseating book on the new/old/modern/ surprising "rules" for sleeping, eating, pooping, and playing by authors whom we have never even met.

The truth is, with families more spread out and nuclear than ever, we no longer have a strong network of hand-me-down wisdom upon which to rely. Most of us don't help bring up our five younger siblings and ten younger cousins anymore. We don't have our mothers and aunts around to show us how to bathe a newborn or cut his nails. Our first brush with the reality of a human baby is often with our own, after we have been unceremoniously discharged from a hospital just two or three days postpartum.

This loss of collective wisdom seems to have caused a level of anxiety that splits our seams. We feel as though we have been left to fend for ourselves. A pediatrician I know told me a story about a woman who called in the middle of the night asking if she should wake her infant to change his poopy diaper. That is how alone we feel.

So we glom on to whatever works for us and feel compelled either to publicly justify our every decision in the face of others' different methods or foist our hard-earned wisdom upon anyone who, in our narrow estimation, might need it.

Let's face it. We are all experts in over-generalizing based on our own experiences. And because everyone has either parented or, at the very least, been parented, we are chock full of anecdotal evidence to support our specious claims. *We actually believe we are qualified to critique your mothering.*

But who could possibly drink from the fire hose of advice shooting in every direction? *You need to read the Baby Whisperer. Ferberize him! Dr. Sears. No, Dr. Spock! NO, DR. OZ! La Leche League would not approve. The new basics. The old basics. Have you tried ear plugs?*

Ack! Shut. Up. All of you.

From now on, if you see me on the street doing something with my son that you would never do, please don't take it

personally. In these times of anxiety and perpetual chatter, sometimes silence is golden.

———————

Debra Cole is a freelance writer, blogger, and mother. She lives in Brooklyn with an impatient toddler, a patient husband, and a neurotic corgi. Once, in the sleepless days of her son's first weeks, she caught her husband beaming while she was nursing. You are a very good Moo Cow, he said, kissing her on the head. Rather than be offended, she embraced the moniker, and a nickname was born. Urban Moo Cow chronicles her transition to motherhood through humorous anecdotes and thoughtful analysis of the issues we face as parents in today's society. Her work has been featured on such sites as BlogHer, Scary Mommy, and Mamapedia.

As Poop Would Have It

By Natasha Peter
Epic Mommy Adventures

*B*eing a mom has been the single most difficult thing that I have ever done in my thirty short years of life. Honestly, I have those moments where I wonder, "What the heck did I get myself into?" Then there are those moments (basically, the majority of the time) where I can't imagine life without my son. Being a single mom, I get to experience and enjoy all of the moments that would normally be shared with a partner. But there's a downside to that, too; you have to clean up all the messes on your own, when it would have been shared with the other person in the relationship.

Disclaimer: This is not one of those cute moments where you say "Awww." Well, there is an awww moment, but this is one of those moments where you really may want to consider whether or not you should venture deeper. It is a poop story, after all, so I have to make sure to warn you.

Before I became a mom, I couldn't mentally deal with bodily fluids, especially having to clean them up. There's just something about them that set me on edge. I loved having kids around me, but changing their diapers and having them pee on me or having to clean up poop from their legs and shoes—let's just say it wasn't something that I enjoyed. For a while, I didn't even want children—then boom, my son came along.

When my son was born and I soon thereafter became a single mom, I knew that I had to change my thinking. My views on pee and poop had to be a thing of the past. My son was all mine, and there was no one to push this difficult job of cleaning up bodily fluids onto. There was no way that I was going to have a child, especially a little boy, and not get used to having to change diapers, deal with loads of drool, or get peed on. I learned very early on that my son would be a challenge with this particular issue. I knew that I would have my work ahead of me.

But why oh why do I have to clean up pee and poop from my foot and the carpet? Yes, you read that right. My son pees and poops on the carpet.

I swear this little boy is a nudist. But I can't completely blame him for it, as I was the same exact way when I was a child. To be completely honest, I hate clothes to this day. So I'll have to blame myself for the things he ends up doing while running around in the nude.

My son has no issue with going buck naked. I'm sure there is some freedom to running around in the nude with the wind touching every part of your body. And I say this, because that's always what he does when he takes off his clothes. He goes running through the house, laughing and giggling the entire way. For a while, I had to watch him intently when I had friends over. He would disappear for a moment and return completely unclothed, running through the house, waving at all my friends, and saying, "Hi!"

Some of my friends were completely shocked, but others found it amusing. Personally, I laughed every time by turning my head and walking out of the room. I couldn't let him see me smile; he would think that his nudity was acceptable.

The nudity went on for some time, when one day I noticed a change in his activities. He wouldn't only get naked, he would then pee and poop on the floor. *What the heck?* I would talk to him, yell at him, punish him, everything—but he would continue to do his business wherever.

My meltdown occurred on a Saturday morning in the first week of this new phase. I had stepped in so much poop that week, I had just had it. Who wants to step in poop every day for a freaking week?

On that momentous day, I left my son in the living room watching television as I went to take a quick shower. When I returned, I noticed the distinct smell of poop in the air. I called out to my son, "Did you poo-poo?" All I heard was giggling. Before I could register that something was up, I felt the wet spot and the squish. I prayed that it wasn't what it felt like and that the giggling that I heard in the distance was not my son taking pride in what he had done. As I picked up my foot and saw the poop dripping off, I knew that things were going downhill.

I walked further into the living room to find that the poop on the floor and on my foot were the least of my concerns. There was poop all over the carpet, the TV console, and the sofa, and my son was sitting behind the sofa trying to get poop off of his little Big Wheel ride-on. He was giggling uncontrollably, and I just completely broke down.

I sat on the floor, possibly right in the poop I had just stepped in, and cried hysterically. I couldn't handle the fact that my son had made this crazy mess. I also balked at the reality that I had to be the one to clean it up. *What did I do to deserve this? Was I such a horrible mother that he felt that he had to punish me with these pooping episodes?*

In the previous days, I had completely snapped and yelled at him for making a mess. After realizing that it was wrong to snap at him like that, I had finally decided to have a conversation with him to make him understand why his actions were very bad. It didn't seem to help since, every day that week, he continued to do the same thing. The only difference was that the situation got increasingly worse by the day. I wondered how I would ever get out of this predicament. When would my son grow out of this phase? Because I knew I couldn't handle it anymore.

After I sobbed uncontrollably for about twenty minutes, my son finally made his way over to me. I'm sure he was sitting there all that time trying to figure out what could be wrong with me and how to approach me. He was calling me and trying to get a hug. I think he realized how much the poop bothered me and was trying to fix it. Without thinking, I picked him up and gave him a big hug. He hugged me back just as tightly, while laying his beautiful little head on my shoulder. I had just enough time to realize what I had done when I felt the poop dripping down his hands, legs, and onto the floor. My tears turned to laughter—a mixture of hysterics and giggles. My son started laughing with me, which made me open my eyes and see the room again, which turned my laughter right back into tears.

After another ten minutes of tears, I finally decided that hysterics would not solve anything. I stood up thinking how silly I looked and carried my son to the bathroom where we both jumped into the shower. We laughed and played in the tub, then finally we got out and went into the bedroom to get dressed. I got us both dressed and we lay on the bed to watch some television. I was just not ready to clean up that mess. I hoped that once I came out of the bedroom, the mess would be clean. Delusional, yes, but I was just not ready to face the music.

We slowly drifted off to sleep.

I awoke to a clinking sound that was obviously the handle on the toilet and the tell-tale sound of flushing. I looked next to me and my son was gone. Oh crap! What was he up to? I got up and looked around, hoping that my son would be on the floor or somewhere nearby and not in the bathroom.

I got up, still somewhat in a daze, and found a sight slightly worse than poop smeared all over the living room. I know how crazy that sounds, but it's the truth. My son was trying to clean up his mess in the living room using toilet paper. As he finished wiping up some of the mess in the living room, he threw the toilet paper in the toilet and was attempting to flush it down.

Unfortunately, there were at least two rolls of paper in the toilet by now, causing the toilet to become backed up. There was now water, toilet paper, and traces of poop all over my bathroom. *Could this day get any worse?* And there was my lil' man with a big grin on his face, showing pride in the help that he was offering to me.

I started shaking uncontrollably. I wasn't sure whether to scream, yell, laugh, or cry. My entire house was a mess. Although it was absolutely adorable that he was trying to help, it created a bigger mess in the end. I was nervous about the amount of water that was on the floor in the bathroom. Plus, it was leaking all over the living room carpet. I decided to just accept the situation.

My son made a mess, yes, and I lost my mind for a little bit, yes. I had to face the fact that I was a single mom, and I had to clean up the mess myself. So I rolled up my sleeves. My son was happy to help me clean. I think that he was nervous about watching me going into hysterics again. I cleaned up the floor while my son held a plastic bag open so I could put of all of the dirty paper towels into it.

I knew I would need to buy a new sofa and loveseat, and I had to get my carpet cleaned, but it was a start to ensuring that all of the poop was cleaned up. After about two hours, everything was cleaned and we took yet another shower. I felt so disgusted by the amount of poop that I needed a moment where I felt clean and refreshed. Honestly, thinking about it again makes me really want to take another shower ... right now.

After that day, my son never again took off his diaper or ran around the house spreading his poop. He had occasions where he would pee on the floor, but never again did he poop on the carpets. I really believe that my reaction to the sight threw him off and he didn't know how to handle it. That is when we finally decided to take a chance on potty-training. We're still trying to successfully achieve that goal, but I know that it will come in time.

Hailing from the beautiful island of St. Croix, Natasha Peter dedicates her days as a consultant and pursuing her Masters of Science in Project Management. Her first, and most important, job is being a single mom to her rambunctious two-year-old toddler son. Natasha is also the writer and editor of Epic Mommy Adventures, a blog focused on single parenthood, co-parenting, dating, toddler eats, co-sleeping, work/ life balance, quality time, and so much more. She also contributes to numerous other blogs and communities around a number of diverse issues.

Soccer Tots: It's Not for Everybody

By Kristi Rieger Campbell
Finding Ninee

When I was pregnant, I planned on going back to work after three months of maternity leave, with my newborn tucked safely in a daycare facility. It's what the moms I knew did. At least, the cool ones went back to work, or, were at least convinced that they would once they actually had kids. I was friendly with a few co-workers' wives, who stayed at home with their children, but it felt, to me, like they were missing out by not working. Work was extremely fulfilling for me, and I was convinced that I would never be a stay-at-home mother.

In the way in which all "I will never" beliefs go, I proved myself wrong by quitting my job about four minutes after my son, Tucker, was born. I couldn't imagine letting anybody else look after him. I experienced the strange new-mom duality of feeling like nobody could possibly know how to hold him correctly other than me, while simultaneously wondering what the hell was wrong with me because I couldn't even figure out breastfeeding. It was such a basic instinct; even the dumbest of mammals figure it out on a daily basis and yet, I couldn't make it work.

My husband was kind enough to suggest that my boobs were simply too big for our tiny man's mouth. I'd have smacked him for that, but wondered the same thing myself. There's nothing quite as disconcerting as looking down and realizing that your once normal-seeming body part is now a bizarre inflated alien and is, in fact, larger than your kid's entire head.

Thankfully, I did figure it out after a few days and ended up successfully breastfeeding for more than a year. During that time, without my career to ground me, and determined to totally rock the new mom thing, I did what I knew in my gut to be the best thing for my son and for myself. For about six months, I pretty much did nothing but join a lame mom's group, go on a lot of walks, and take the advice of "sleep when the baby sleeps" to a prize-winning level.

At some point, after Tucker became mobile and began to sleep through the night, I managed to get enough sleep each evening to wake up one day and realize that I was beyond bored. I briefly considered going back to work but knew that I no longer had it in me to work sixty to seventy hours each week. I knew that I'd freak out about traveling without my little boy and, if I'm honest, I knew that I really preferred the option of passing out at three o'clock in the afternoon—the same time that Tucker did.

But I was bored. Also, I worried that my son was the unluckiest boy on the planet because surely other mothers were better at enjoying floor-mat time and reading mindless rhyming books out loud over and over and over again. So, I fell back on what I'd learned from my own parents growing up. "Be a joiner! Find activities to participate in and make friends. Your kid will make friends and you'll all bond for life!"

I signed up, all right. I signed up for Mommy and Me swim classes, a Wiggles and Giggles class, and countless others with equally adorable and deceptive names. Some of them were almost fun. There was an Abracadoodles art class that I have a few fond memories of.

But none were as awesome-sounding as Soccer Tots. Previous classes were merely a fill-in for my true imagined perfect activity to represent little boyness. I loved soccer practice as a kid and was convinced that my kid would be the cutest little soccer ball kickin' dude ever. I imagined that he'd rock soccer like nobody's

business, that I'd find mom friends, and be able to rest each night knowing that I'd done my part in participating in something productive and stimulating for my baby.

During each class, the coaches created these fun obstacle courses for the kids, where they would first jump over a line of noodles, then crawl through a tunnel, then run through stacks of cones, and finally get a ball and shoot a goal. *Sounds fun, right?*

It wasn't. At least, it wasn't fun for my son; which meant that it wasn't fun for me, either. If the activity wasn't one that Tucker *wildly* enjoyed, he wouldn't participate in it at all, preferring to run or to find the patch of light on the field coming from a sky-light. Still determined, I often worked up a sweat, literally guiding Tucker through the obstacle courses. I'd take his arms and jump him over the noodles, while fighting with him to not pick them up and run away with them. I'd help him to run around the cones, while frantically picking them up, because he'd decided that it was much more fun to kick them down than to weave among them. It was frustrating and heart wrenching for me to watch other children my son's age complete these basic courses so much better than he did. Still too thick-headed to give up, after six months, I enrolled him in a soccer class with a younger group of children, thinking his skill levels might be more evenly matched to theirs.

They weren't. I tried to make Soccer Tots fun for a full year. That entire year was full of noticing increasingly alarming differences between my son and his peers. During that time, we'd begun evaluations and had begun to meet with doctors in an attempt to learn what was going on with Tucker's behavior and his speech and language delay. We were convinced that our little boy wasn't autistic while simultaneously watching him exhibit what I know now to be behaviors that put him on the autism spectrum.

Back then, though, I still hadn't given up the dream of soccer working for us. I had witnessed enough moments when he did enjoy class to stick with it. After all, he was incredibly engaged when the activity was popping bubbles using only his feet and his head.

Then, we had a day when he wasn't engaged in anything. During circle time, my son was off and running toward a tiny gap in the wall, wanting me to play hide-and-seek with him. During the noodle river while other children—younger than him—dribbled the soccer ball to a tunnel, climbed through it, and then scored a goal once out, my son was disruptively dumping a bucket of baseballs he found near the bleachers left over from the class before us. That day, a couple of moms gave me "The Look." You know the one. It says, "Control your son," while also disarming you because it comes with a half-assed smile.

That was the day that we didn't linger after class under the guise of finishing our snacks and water, secretly hoping one of the moms would want to talk to us and maybe even exchange a phone number. That day, I was embarrassed. I high-tailed it out of there, Tucker in tow, got to the parking lot, and, of course, dropped my keys on the ground. I wiped the sweat from my brow that had not yet dried from my efforts to make Soccer Tots fun. I strapped him into his car seat, and got pissed. I got *really pissed.*

I screamed at my little boy, "*What's wrong with you?*"

He immediately began crying, and I felt like the biggest meanie, mean, asshole that's ever been lucky enough to hear the word "mom" come from a little boy's mouth.

We quit soccer that day. I never even called to request a refund for the remaining classes. I swore to myself and to my son that I would never again ask him what was wrong with him. I still have a hard time reliving that moment without a giant dose of guilt and tears. *What's wrong with him? Jesus. What the hell is wrong with me? I screamed at my forever favorite and I made him cry.*

Asking my son "What's wrong with you?" is one of the most regrettable things that I've done. Looking at the kid I know now, versus the kid I imagined him to be back then, I can't believe I even put him through that soccer shit in the first place.

To my darling son Tucker,

I'm sorry. I'm sorry that I ever expected you to act "normal." I didn't realize that you wanting to jump in a patch of light is something that is caused by a neurological something-or-other in your brain. I didn't realize that you were having fun in your own way, by your own rules, and that a soccer class, with expected conformity, wasn't going to give you the joy that it gave me as a child. You are normal. You are normal and you are different. You are not typical. You are perfect. You are perfect, exactly as you are.

My darling son ... I believe in you. I believe in your power to change the world and to make everybody more empathetic and light. I will never again try to fit your star-shaped self into a circle-shaped hole. I promise.

And I'll never say the words, "What's wrong with you?" to anybody, ever again.

Love,
Mom

———

Kristi Rieger Campbell is a semi-lapsed career woman with about eighteen years of marketing experience in a variety of national and global technology companies. More recently, she was a co-host on a hilarious (and under-funded) weekly radio show. Once her son was born, she became the mom who almost always leaves the house in either flip-flops or Uggs, depending on the weather. While she does work part-time, her passion is writing and drawing really stupid-looking pictures for her blog, Finding Ninee. Finding Ninee (pronounced nine-ee for her son's pronunciation of the word airplane) started due to a memoir, abandoned when Kristi read that a publisher would rather shave a cat than read another. Its primary focus is to find and provide humor and support in a "Middle World"; one where the autism spectrum exists, but a diagnosis does not.

BONUS #2

Epic Celebrity Meltdowns

By Lisa Witherspoon

This book is chock full of mothering meltdowns that, at the time, probably seemed monumental. We can take comfort, however, in the knowledge that even celebrity moms have meltdowns. Despite their fame, fortune, and ability to hire unlimited nannies and assistants, it seems they frequently misstep just like the rest of us. Unfortunately for them, their meltdowns are usually caught on camera and splattered all over the front pages of the tabloids. Hopefully their legendary mothering mishaps will make the rest of us feel a little better about our minor offenses. Here's a list of some of the worst celebrity mommy meltdowns ever!

The Mother of All Mommy Meltdowns Award goes to Joan Crawford. Portrayed by Faye Dunaway in the 1981 movie *Mommie Dearest*, Crawford has a multitude of meltdowns. One of the most memorable depicts her frantically cutting off her daughter Christina's hair when she finds out that she is playing with her make-up and believes the little girl is making fun of her. Of course, everyone has heard of the scene where Crawford finds her daughter's expensive dresses hanging on wire hangers and begins screaming "No more wire hangers!" She then proceeds to tear all the dresses from the closet and beats her daughter with one of the hangers she loathes so much. It truly is difficult and painful to watch her meltdowns portrayed on the big screen.

Second place is awarded to Britney Spears. Spears, of course, rose to fame as a pop music icon in the late 1990s. In 2004, she married Kevin Federline and they had two sons in rather rapid succession. After the couple divorced in 2006, Spears spiraled into an epic meltdown. The paparazzi caught pictures of her partying and appearing severely intoxicated. Who could forget the image of her with her shaved head? She lost physical custody of her two sons in October 2007. In early January 2008, she was hospitalized for a mental evaluation and lost visitation rights to her children. For now, it seems that rehab was successful for Spears. She has regained rights to visit with her sons and her career is on the mend.

Next up is Kris Jenner, the matriarch of the Kardashian clan. She should be cited for the most horrendous moral meltdown in all of mothering history. Have you ever wondered why this Kardashian family is so famous? Well, it all started with a homemade "adult film" starring Kris's daughter Kim Kardashian. The film was leaked and became very popular which catapulted Kim (and the family) to stardom. Here's the meltdown part: it has recently been reported that mom, Kris, actually directed the flick and negotiated the deal to sell it to a production company for public release! As if that wasn't enough, it is no secret that Kris Jenner serves as "momager" for her daughters' modeling careers. She exploits them in every way possible to make a buck and has been referred to as the ultimate pimp—only her "clients" are her own daughters! This definitely qualifies as a monumental meltdown of mothering ethics.

Also making the list is Brooke Mueller. Don't know who she is? She has been described as a "socialite, occasional actress, and real estate broker." You probably know her best as Charlie Sheen's third wife. They were married in 2008 and had twin sons in 2009. Sheen filed for divorce in 2010. After that, there were custody disputes and accusations of domestic violence. At one point, social services removed the children from Sheen after Mueller filed for a restraining order and stated that she

thought Sheen was "insane." Then, in 2012, Mueller was placed on involuntary psychiatric hold and later admitted to the Betty Ford Clinic for drug addiction. And the children? Well, this couple is so full of crazy that a judge actually awarded custody of the twin boys to Sheen's *other* ex-wife, Denise Richards. That's one messed up, full-on family meltdown!

Next up is Kate Moss. Her meltdown happened when, in 2005, she went on a cocaine binge with her then rocker boyfriend and it was splayed all over the front page of *The Daily Mirror*, a British tabloid. She never lost custody of her daughter who was two at the time, although she did miss her third birthday party while doing a stint in rehab. Moss' career experienced a colossal meltdown, as she lost many endorsements from major companies including H&M, Burberry, and Rimmel as a result of the scandal.

Another notable celebrity mom who has a history meltdowns is Courtney Love. She's the rocker who married fellow rocker Kurt Cobain in 1992. They had one daughter, Frances Bean. In 2009, Bean actually filed for a restraining order against her mother as a result of repeated meltdowns that involved telephone screaming matches, Twitter rants, and allegations of domestic abuse. The two are now reportedly taking some very small steps toward reconciling this mother-daughter relationship meltdown.

Finishing out the list is Reese Witherspoon, who recently made headlines in April, 2013, when she was arrested for disorderly conduct. Reese was in a car with her husband when he was pulled over. He was subsequently arrested and charged with DUI. We all know that our husbands are kind of like additional kids and it is only natural to become upset when one of our kids is accused of a crime, right? Well, in a statement later released by the actress, she said when she saw her husband being arrested, she "literally panicked." This led her to be verbally abusive to the police officer involved. She refused to stay in the car as directed, told him she was pregnant (not true), and ranted

"Don't you know who I am?" She has apologized and admitted that the whole thing was a terribly embarrassing meltdown.

The fact is, we are all human and we all make mistakes. Most of us aren't famous, so we don't have to worry about being followed by the paparazzi and, normally, our blunders don't make the headlines. In our hearts and minds, though, they sometimes seem monumental. Hopefully, these little glimpses of some truly epic meltdowns will put even our worst mommy moments into perspective!

All information included in this list has been obtained from the following sources: Wikipedia, People, Your Tango, Hollywood Reporter, and Rolling Out.

Do Wedding Rings Sink or Swim?

By Tamara Bowman
Tamara (Like) Camera

When it was time to plan our wedding, I nearly drowned in the details. Writing our own vows? I did my brainstorming on the top of Buena Vista Park in San Francisco with a black wire-rimmed notebook and a BIC pen. Planning the music? I spent hours making play lists. Food? I could dig that. We had our tasting on an east coast trip to our wedding venue in Vermont where we sat and feasted like kings with our whole extended family. When one of the dishes on display had cilantro in it, the three super tasters at the table who hate cilantro practically banged their fists on the table and demanded it be taken away. That actually wasn't our finest moment.

However, I was *there.* I was opinionated. I was planning. Surprisingly, they let us come back and have our wedding day.

I'm not a diligent person. I'm sloppy at best. I color outside the lines. My handwriting is terrible. I sew in jagged lines (and not on purpose), and I can't knit without getting everything tangled on the floor. Usually I give up soon after.

When things get too crafty or detailed, rather than introspective and open-ended, I start to panic and shut down. My husband, Cassidy, took care of so many details in our self-planned wedding. He designed the style of the save the dates and came up with the unique pop-up idea for our invitations. He planned paper stock and printing. He printed *LOST* themed labels from the Internet and put them around Bell jars and candy. He digitally designed the cover and layout of our wedding program. Oh sure, I wrote my head and heart off in the "We Remember" section, as well as the introductions to every single member of the bridal party. That was writing. That was different. The only detail left to me was to work on our wedding rings with the jeweler we had chosen.

That was my baby. As they say, "You had one job! ONE job!"

The rings were platinum with both of our birthstones, rubies and diamonds, spaced around the outside of the bands. On the inside of the bands, we had them engraved with lyrics from Dire Straits' haunting "Romeo and Juliet" song. Mine said, "YOU AND ME BABE ..." and his said, "HOW ABOUT IT?" I was so proud of myself. When the rings arrived a month before our wedding, it was all I could do not to wear mine all the time. I was superstitious about wearing my ring before the ceremony, but there was one moment when I slipped it on and stood under a San Francisco sunset to watch it gleam. After that I waited until the ring exchange at our ceremony to wear it for good.

I didn't take my ring off until the very end of my pregnancy with our first child, Scarlet. About two weeks after she was born, I discovered that my fingers had gone back to their original size and I put it back on again. I didn't take it off to swim. I didn't take it off to shower. I did, however, take it off to potty-train my daughter. Here's what happened ...

One sunny spring morning two years ago, we had some time to kill before my older sister was due to arrive from New Jersey for a visit. Scarlet was nearly two years old, and on this rare occasion she informed me that she had to go to the bathroom, rather than just using her diaper as a toilet like every other time. Well, I jumped at the chance. I set her on the little training potty as we often did—watching Jerry Garcia to help her move her bowels along. (Try it! It works!) Despite the amazing entertainment, she was getting a little restless. She wanted to hug me, which was awkward to do while she was sitting on her little toilet.

I did it anyway, because how could I not, really? As we broke our hug, she expressed interest in my wedding ring—the one I NEVER take off, right? Even though my husband was out doing errands, I looked around sheepishly, making sure no one could see me give my not even two-year-old a very expensive wedding ring. Not to mention, I didn't want the invisible and judgmental audience to see that I potty-trained my daughter to Jerry Garcia. That invisible and judgmental audience may also have noted me giving a choking-sized object to a toddler, but you'd have to know my daughter first. She has always been a careful and gentle little human. She was well past the oral stage and only put food, drinks, and her thumb into her mouth. So giving her my wedding ring was a cinch, right?

My worries about my invisible and judgmental audience faded into the wings of my living room as we had a victory. She suddenly stood up and shouted, "Poop in the potty!" I did a victory dance. She did a victory dance. I rushed her and the potty upstairs to flush the contents down the real toilet. Then I cleaned her up and took her downstairs. Cookies were doled out. We began the "You pooped in the potty" song and dance again when Cassidy came home to hear of the good news, and then we went outside to play.

It was one of those beautifully perfect days in early spring—sunny with blue sky and puffy clouds, a cool breeze, and no humidity. It was outside in the sunshine that I first noticed my naked left hand. In all of the pooping excitement, I had forgotten that Scarlet was holding my ring while she was on her baby toilet. My stomach sank. I started to panic. I looked (or so I thought) everywhere in the living room and upstairs. I even asked Scarlet where the ring was. She just mimicked me, and repeated, "Where did ring go?" while looking under the coffee table. It wasn't there. As I tore apart the living room and threw couches and pillows everywhere, she followed me like a little parrot, "Where did ring go? Where did ring go?"

I did not tell Cassidy what had happened. He was in the house, but I was hiding my panic. I was reeling it in. By now I had deduced EXACTLY what had happened. While pooping to Jerry Garcia, Scarlet dropped my beloved wedding ring into her toilet. Then, she pooped on top of it. Naturally. Then when I ran upstairs to flush down the poop, I forgot about the ring and flushed it down the toilet. I was 110 percent sure of this. To me, it was pure logic. You know what I didn't do? Tell Cassidy. Or cry. Or react. I shut my terror and horror inside whenever he was around.

I didn't call the landlord or the plumber either. My sister arrived and I told her what had happened. I both laughed and cried with her over the ridiculousness of losing my prized wedding ring in my toddler's poop and flushing it down the toilet. My sister was comforting and told me I had lost a material object and not a living being. I was comforted ... temporarily. I still didn't tell Cassidy. I didn't know how he'd react with my sister there, and I didn't want her in the middle of any tension.

So I did some pretty illogical things. I melted down inside for two days. I hid my left hand. The icing on the cake was when I emailed our amazing L.A.-based jeweler to ask if him he still had the design plans for our wedding ring. He did, and he was very understanding about my pain. I was about to be very largely in debt. I'm sure I didn't have $100 to my name, much less over $1,000, but I was going ahead with this plan. I told a few friends and they seemed sympathetic but were probably amused. I mean, how could you not be? Jerry Garcia? Poop? Wedding rings down the toilet? Fantastic.

The jeweler wrote that he would go ahead with the plans, but only with my blessing. It was go time. I sat and stared at the computer screen. I could feel two days of intense fear and sadness bubbling to the surface. Cassidy chose that exact time to come home from work to find me sitting at the computer with my head deeply buried in my hands. "What on earth is wrong?" he asked, and that was the trigger, the invitation, for every emotion

I had reeled in for the last two days. It started with quivering lips. Then the tears. Then the full-on, body-wracking sobs. He looked astonished and freaked out. He must have thought the worst. I saw his eyes dart everywhere and anywhere (but not at my left hand), until they settled on Scarlet. His brain registered that she was okay, but something was most definitely wrong.

"It's really, really bad," I sobbed. Scarlet was now huddled in the corner in fear. She had never seen me cry and certainly not in this wild and crazed way.

I've never been in Cassidy's head (very sadly), but if the roles had been reversed, I would have conjured up images of deceased loved ones, accidents, or marital affairs. Actually if he had cried and told me, "It's really bad," I'd probably have to sit down and put my head between my knees just to hear the news.

He put his steady hand on my unsteady, flailing arm and said, "Spill it. Now."

Around choked-up and choked-in and choked-out sobs, I said it. Really fast. "I gave my wedding ring to Scarlet to play with. She pooped on it. I flushed it down the toilet. Don't worry because I'm already making the replacement with Ernie, our jeweler. It's going to cost a lot of money, but I figure if I put aside $50 a week from my crappy, part-time job, I'll have it paid for in about a year. Assuming we don't want to eat ever again. Or celebrate Christmas. Or have gas in our cars."

Luckily, at this point, I stopped to take a breath and see his reaction.

He didn't look mad or upset. He looked thoughtful and concerned. "Wait, let me get this straight. You flushed your wedding ring down the toilet with Scarlet's poop?"

"Yes."

"Did you actually see the ring go down the toilet?"

"No."

"So you're basing this theory on what, exactly?"

"She must have dropped it in her own poop, and I flushed it!"

"Did you hear a clink of the ring hitting the porcelain?"

"No."

"So that theory has no basis. The ring has to be in this house. The first thing I'd do is tear apart the living room."

I can't promise I saw the light and realized there was another way. I thought it was an incredible waste of time to search apart the house for a tiny ring that had been flushed down the toilet. I thought it was MUCH more effective to bottle it up inside for two days to the point of a pretty serious meltdown, only to get myself into thousands of dollars of debt.

We started in the living room. We looked under the pillows and then moved apart the sections of the large couch. Under the first couch, we found three of Scarlet's lost books. "Yippee!" she shouted. "But where did ring go?"

Indeed.

Cassidy moved aside a second couch section. There we found a few dust bunnies, a penny, and … a glistening wedding ring. My toilet theory? Totally wrong. I couldn't see the many holes in the story, I suppose. It never occurred to me that what really happened is that Scarlet had become inevitably bored with my shiny ring, because Jerry Garcia was helping to move her bowels along so effectively, that she dropped my ring and it rolled under the couch. Where it sat for days.

I grabbed my ring, jumped up, and threw my arms around Cassidy. Then I ran to call the jeweler to "stop the presses." He was happy for me, too. I was happy for me. Cassidy even bought me ice cream that night to celebrate—to celebrate my ridiculousness. Let's hope I learned something important from this experience. Not only about logic, but also about marriage. If you get yourself into what you think is some serious trouble, tell your spouse sooner rather than later. It may save you over a thousand dollars, as well as days of pain.

I haven't had the likes of a meltdown like that since. Also, I've learned a few things for when we potty-train our son. Jerry Garcia? Yes. Wedding rings? No.

Tamara Bowman is a professional photographer, a mama of two, a writer/blogger at Tamara (Like) Camera, and a nearly professional cookie taster. She has been known to be all four of those things at all hours of the day and night. After two cross-country moves, due to her intense Bi-Coastal Disorder, she lives with her husband, daughter, and son in glorious western Massachusetts. Pets are soon to follow. They like it here and they aren't going anywhere, unless they obtain a winning lottery ticket, in which case they'd also have a home on the west coast for half of the year. Tamara dreams about northern lights, moose, and whales always. She also likes puppies, lattes, and rainbows an awful lot.

Mommy's Money Meltdown

By Rabia Lieber
The Liebers

Money is tight at my house; seems like it always is. On one hand, it seems like we always have just enough money for what we absolutely need. On the other hand, I'm tired of being stressed about every single dollar that comes in or goes out of our bank account. And don't get me wrong, I'm very thankful that my husband and I both have good jobs. In fact, we both work for the state, although in different sectors.

I have been at my current job for two years now. I *love* it! I have a great boss, great co-workers, and a great schedule. I really have nothing to complain about. A lot of people around me complain though, because state workers haven't had a raise in five years. I complain a little on behalf of my husband, because he has been with the state for over five years and his salary has been the same all that time.

Then the state announced raises for employees in the next fiscal year. I was doubly excited because it means that my husband and I both get raises. Even though people around me were grumbling that the raise only covered the increase in health insurance costs, I was still happy about it. I did little, fanciful calculations with my pretty pink calculator to see how much more a year we would get. I doodled with my purple pen on my pretty Post-it notes. How much more a month? How much more a day? Think middle-schooler doodling hearts around initials on a notebook and you'll get pretty close to what I looked like.

Trust me. I wasn't spending all that money in my head. I was just trying it out and fantasizing about putting three slices of meat on a sandwich when I packed my lunch! Or maybe even some lettuce or tomatoes! Be still my heart!

The state was sending out emails and so was my manager. They kept spelling out how these raises would work, who they would affect, and which hoops to jump through to get them. I noticed in these emails that it was hard to tell exactly how much of a raise each person would get. It was a little bit high school logic and math with "if this, then that" statements combined with a Nancy Drew *Choose Your Own Adventure* book.

My husband and I had long romantic talks about the raises. In retrospect, it was more of me offering all kinds of possibilities for how to calculate it and him saying sweet nothings like, "Why don't we just wait and see?" I was starting to get myself all worked up about the possibility of more money that even I knew wasn't going to amount to a whole lot, especially after the new health care costs were factored in.

Then I got an email from my youngest child's daycare. It was disguised as a newsletter about all the fun things that had been going on in the past month. I love reading these newsletters because they do a lot of fun things at this daycare. My son is in the youngest class, so I like to read ahead and see what kinds of things he'll get to do as he gets older.

The last page of the newsletter was the kicker: a form to indicate that tuition prices would be increasing at the end of the summer. No. NO. NO! That money I had been doodling about was about to be taken away. *But how bad could it be, really?* So I will admit to being in a bad mood when I read the notice. My fantasy of sandwiches with lettuce and tomatoes was falling apart right before my eyes. It was through these lenses that I read further. There was a chart—a chart that showed current prices and new prices. Right there next to each other. So easy to read and understand.

When I looked at the chart, I was already mad. It said tuition was going up by $20. Surely it meant $20 a year, right? Or a month? Please let it be $20 a month. Nope! It was $20 a week! ARGH! I can't believe this! Not only is my raise going to go straight to daycare, but this goes beyond that and sticks us further in the hole.

I quickly called my husband, who did not answer the phone (as is usually the case when I call his cell phone while he's at work). I shot off an instant message to a co-worker I had previously commiserated with about lack of funds in our respective households:

"SO MUCH FOR MY RAISE! DAYCARE TUITION IS GOING UP $20 A WEEK!"

Yes, I yelled at him in all capitals. He was out of his office and didn't respond either. I was glad my boss (with whom I'm sharing an office for the summer due to construction) was not around. He is a very kind and empathetic man. If he had seen my face at that instant, he would have asked me what was wrong. And then I would have cried all over the office. As it was, I did sit at my desk and fume for quite a while. I did more math with my pretty pink calculator, except this time I wrote numbers on a Post-it note in black ink, instead of purple. Think of that same middle-schooler's notebook after she gets dumped—the day before prom! ARGH!

I was mad, broke, stuck at work, and totally unable to do anything about the situation. Just looking at that dumb chart made me want to punch right through the computer screen. But I couldn't do *that* because then I'd probably have to pay for it, my co-workers would think I was a spaz, and it would likely just hurt my hand anyway.

So I got up and walked down to the front of the building to check the mail. I got a drink of water, went to the bathroom, and tried to calm down. *Why can't we ever get ahead?* And when I had wasted as much time as I thought prudent, I went back to my office. I pulled up that stupid chart and started to click the little red X in the corner. And something caught my eye. The headings on the chart. One definitely said "new full-time rate." The other one, however, didn't say "previous rate" like I thought it had. It said "sibling rate"—as in, they offer a discount of $20 to anyone who has more than one child enrolled.

I looked at the new rate and my brain buzzed around a bit on that number. Then I looked up my spreadsheet where I keep track of my payments. Oh. OH. OH! The difference ... only $2 a week! We aren't going to the poor house (yet)! Two dollars a week I can handle. That's not huge. It's less than our raises will be, anyway! Phew! I was so relieved!

And then my co-worker instant messaged me, "That sucks!"

What? What sucks? Oh! Yeah, that meltdown I had about the daycare tuition. "Um ... actually I read the email wrong. It's only $2 a week, not $20."

"Oh. Well that's better," he replied.

"Yep!"

And I was almost giddy again with new-found money. Sandwiches! With three slices of ham! And tomatoes! And lettuce! And maybe even pickles and two different kinds of cheese!

And it began to seem a bit funny to me, how stressed I was over it. Not that a $20 hike in daycare tuition would be something we could just handle without a care but, now that it was a big mistake on my part, I was laughing at myself.

So I grinned when I told the daycare director about it at pick-up time. I actually paused for a minute to watch the look on her face when she thought that she had mistyped something. Then I emphatically assured her that it was entirely my fault and not hers at all. Then we laughed about it together.

I picked up the kids, went home, and checked the mail. You know, all the usual stuff. I sat down to go through the contents of the mailbox before I started dinner. There was an envelope from Sallie Mae in there. I knew it couldn't be a bill because we have it paid automatically by the bank. I hesitantly opened it up and

it said that our payment amount was changing. It gave the new amount, but not the old amount. No. NO. NO! Not this again! Twice in one day?! You have got to be kidding me.

So I fired up the browser and checked out our online banking to see how much of a difference there would be. I scrolled and scrolled, feeling my stress levels rising again. And I found it! The difference? Thirty cents! It was going down! Thirty whole cents a month!

And it was about this time that my husband returned my frantic call from earlier. "What's wrong?" he asked.

"Oh, nothing. Our daycare bill is going up by $2 a week. But our student loan bill is going down by $0.30 a month. No big deal."

And somehow we always seem to have exactly as much as we need.

Rabia Lieber is the Co-Executive Director and Chief Van Operator in the Lieber household. She's a full-time working mom of three (one girl and two boys) who blogs in her "spare" time ... whatever that is! She's been married to her husband, Ken, for twelve years and together they are trying to teach their children to pretend they have manners in public, appreciate all things geek, and gracefully avoid meltdowns before bedtime and in the grocery store. She blogs about family life and other things that strike her fancy over at The Liebers.

Sass Rhymes With ...

By Rachel Demas
Tao of Poop

*C*lass. Another word comes to mind. That word applies too. I'm talking about the time I *lost* my class in the face of my two-year-old's bedtime sass.

Ironically, I hadn't had a meltdown during the seventeen months that my daughter was waking up hourly every night. I'd had my moments. Moments are different from meltdowns. Meltdowns require a certain amplitude and duration.

It was the sass. My daughter got me with her sass.

The particular bedtime in question started innocently enough. Claire was consistently sleeping through the night (hooray). We had established a good bedtime routine too: bath, stories, lights out.

We co-sleep, so I was lying in our bed while Claire rested in her side-car crib, minus the railing. The slow wind down to sleep began. She babbled, rolled around, and requested to hold my hand.

She started licking it.

What is she doing, I thought. *That's a new move.*

I pulled my hand away without saying a word. She pounced on it, flinging her body off her crib, and onto me and the bed.

"Hmmm?" I thought. She'd rarely breached the invisible barrier between her crib and our bed. I was flummoxed.

I carefully moved her body back to the bed. In my head, I called upon a higher power. "Now, what do I do, Dr. Sears? I don't remember this chapter of the book."

We repeated the crib/bed dance several times, at which point Claire got the bright idea that she and Mommy were playing a game instead of sleeping.

"STOP! It's time for rest, not time to play," I said.

I put one forearm down the length of her torso to block her attacks, while I continued to contemplate the wisdom of our decision to practice Attachment Parenting. My counter worked … until …

The stakes of the game were raised. Claire began kicking around and over my arm—hard. Her blows hit me in any area where I could not protect myself with outstretched hands. I imagined our bedroom resembling a scene from *The Exorcist*.

"I DON'T LIKE BEING KICKED, CLAIRE. STOP. YOU'RE HURTING ME!" I beseeched.

I longed for an extra set of hands and a straitjacket for my daughter. I wished that we had done "Cry It Out" long ago. I began to question the "gentle" approach to sleep. Dr. Sears probably hadn't said a word about it being gentle for parents, but still …

Laughter … more kicking … more laughter. Claire was taunting me. Adding insult to injury, she had zero empathy for the pain she was inflicting on me.

That one-two punch is what I call sass.

"DO YOU WANT ME TO TURN THE CRIB AROUND?" I yelled, my patience and options diminishing.

"YES!" she screamed at me. My eyes had adjusted to the dark. I could see the mocking, defiant grin that matched her satanic giggle.

"If I turn the crib around, there's no more kicking and there will be no more mama," I desperately offered, in the vain hope that my threat would be enough to stop her assault.

"TURN. THE. CRIB. AROUND," she yelled. With each finely-enunciated, contemptuous word, a blow landed squarely on my body.

I'd had it. I had no choice but to show her who was boss. She'd backed me into a corner, really. Then there was that thing called my white-hot rage at being defied. All the elements necessary for a meltdown were now complete.

I grabbed her from the crib and deposited her on the floor next to the bed. Now, what was I going to do?

The crib was wedged tightly between the wall and the box spring and mattress on the floor. It was tight on purpose so Claire couldn't fall through the crack.

I had no plan. I did have a point to make.

I stood on the bed, grabbed one end of the crib, and pulled. Now the crib was wedged cock-eyed between the wall and the side of our mattress. I moved to the other side of the crib and pulled harder. Two of its four legs came off the ground.

This damn crib was as defiant as my daughter. I had found a new foe, one worthy of Claire and Dr. Sears.

I jumped off the bed and picked up the mattress at a 45-degree angle and flung it to one side. I shoved the unyielding box spring, jimmied the crib up onto the box spring, and rotated the crib around.

All the while, I rambled on to no one in particular like a possessed, crazy woman, as Claire watched from the side of the bed. I didn't even have the presence of mind to see her reaction. Was she crying? Did she think me insane? Was she scared? Maybe she felt a combination of all three.

In under ten minutes, I had completed the task—with my daughter in a heap on the other side of the railing, wailing at my behavior and her new jail cell.

Do you know how unwieldy a mattress is? Do you know how hard it is to budge a box spring? I was endowed with superhuman strength that night, like the proverbial mother who lifts a car to save her child trapped underneath.

As I look back on my bedtime meltdown, I can't believe the contrast of that *one* night to my seventeen months of sleep deprivation. During those seventeen long months, I'd patiently risen above my own pain to help my daughter learn how to fall asleep. It may have felt like she was to blame for my sheer and utter zombie-like state, but I knew it wasn't her fault.

Looking back from the vantage point of relative sanity, I don't regret our sleeping decisions either. I would do it all over again, despite my protestations to the Attachment Parenting gods that night. Indeed, now that I've gotten my wits about me again, I'd like to take this moment to publicly apologize to Dr. Sears and my daughter.

Of course, I wish I could take that night back. But within it lay another hallmark of a meltdown. I was not thinking clearly while losing my mind. I reacted from a small, impotent place inside of me.

In other words, I took the sass personally.

I was kind of in shock, too. Did you know a barely two-year-old was capable of such sass? I didn't. Now I know better.

I know what my daughter is capable of doing. I know which of my buttons she is capable of pushing. And, what's most humbling, I know how capable I am of reacting to having my buttons pushed by her.

On a positive note, I also know I have superhuman strength. I practiced using it for good too. I put the crib back. It's stayed that way since that night, along with my class.

Rachel Demas isn't always engaged in heavy lifting around the house. She balances the brawn with some brain at her blog, Tao of Poop, where she writes about the shock and amazement of being a first-time mom. The star of Tao of Poop is Claire, her delightful and impossible two year old. Making guest appearances are her husband, George, and two cats, Lloyd and Sophia. Please consider this bio your invitation to join this motley cast of characters for one wild and crazy ride.

Lait Pour le Bébé

By Nicole Goodman
Work in Sweats Mama

"*C*est lait pour mon bébé. Où est-il? Où est-il?!" Translation: It's milk for my baby. Where is it? Where is it?!

At the ungodly hour of 4:30 a.m., I choked out those simple words and felt a sick feeling spreading from the pit of my belly to the back of my throat. My tongue tripped over the pronunciation and I blinked back tears, the panic spreading like wildfire.

Yes, those simple words were the beginning of my mother of all meltdowns; a meltdown my daughters weren't even present for, but to which they were inextricably linked.

We can trace the meltdown's origins to 2009, before my oldest was even born. Like most mamas-to-be, I was neck-deep in pregnancy books, magazines, and web sites, researching every aspect of my little miracle's arrival. I followed her progress week by week, telling my husband which piece of produce she was comparable to at that moment. "Honey, she's the size of a kumquat this week!" Seriously, does anyone even know what a kumquat is, much less how big it is?

As part of my fastidious research, I read everything I could get my hands on about breastfeeding. I was determined to feed my baby the way nature intended. Don't worry. I'm not going to get all hippy-dippy, super crunchy on you. Breastfeeding is a personal choice every mother makes based on what's right for her. It just so happens the right choice for me was to breastfeed my babies, come hell or high water. Or cracked nipples and clogged ducts.

So, I did my homework. I talked to my friends. I went to breastfeeding classes. Then my daughter was born, and I realized I didn't have a clue!

But we soldiered on, and after the first awkward, tearful, painful days, we figured it out and never looked back. It wasn't always easy. Did I mention the painful days when it felt like my nipples were being sliced off with a knife?! Nothing natural about that!

But my nipples toughened up, the pain subsided, and we eventually settled into a routine. I had this gig under control, at least until maternity leave was over and I had to go back to work.

And thus began the intimate bonding with my breast pump and the never-ending calculation of milk math. For the non-initiated, milk math is the highly scientific arithmetic a pumping mother does every day to calculate whether she's pumped enough milk to fill the next day's bottles. Don't underestimate the difficulty of simple addition and subtraction when you're sleep deprived and suffering from a major case of mommy brain! Milk math is exponentially harder than geometry, calculus, and statistics combined. I daresay it's even harder than those crazy, advanced math classes my engineer husband took in college. That math doesn't even use numbers, but it still pales in comparison to milk math.

To compound matters, I knew I'd have to take several business trips while I was still breastfeeding. With both girls, I started stockpiling milk right away, taking advantage of early days when my cup(s) literally runneth over.

I'd pump an ounce or two before each feeding, depositing those precious ounces in the milk bank. Eventually I started waking up early every morning and pumping one side before I nursed on the other.

As every breastfeeding mother knows, there's a reason they call it liquid gold. Breast milk is the most valuable commodity

you possess, and every drop is precious. Hooking yourself up to the dairy farm is no picnic, so you guard every droplet like it's the last pint of Ben & Jerry's on the planet.

At some point, every pumping mother experiences the anguish, the agony, and the indescribable horror of watching her liquid gold go down the drain. Or spill on the counter. No matter how it happens, whether it's a slip of the hand or a hole in a freezer bag, witnessing your milk go to waste is worthy of its own epic meltdown.

The first time I spilled milk, I thought I was going to have an aneurysm. My heart was racing. My vision was blurry. My mouth was coated with the metallic tang of blood. My husband rushed to my side to see why I had cried out, why I was sobbing uncontrollably.

"It's ok. It's not even an ounce." Not the right thing for him to say. Not by a long shot. In fact, I don't know if there is a right thing to say. The only viable options are either embrace your blubbering wife in your arms and let her wail against the unjust universe that would do this unspeakable thing to her, or turn on your heel and run for the hills.

If a tiny spill could reduce me to a hyperventilating mess, can you imagine how I felt when faced with losing a week's worth of milk? Yeah, it wasn't pretty. Whoever coined the phrase "don't cry over spilled milk" never lactated, that's for damn sure!

After my near-stroke experience, I implemented a meticulous 47-step transfer process, which included human sacrifice (a.k.a. pumping) and a series of fervent incantations, to make sure every precious drop made it to the freezer unscathed.

When it was time for my first business trip, there were enough freezer bags to carry my daughter through my absence. Of course, there's no rest for the weary. I packed my pump and its 15,000 accoutrements so I could keep up my supply and replenish the depleted stock. Thus began my trials and tribulations with pumping on the go … and in the air.

Over the course of the two combined years I nursed my daughters, I went on seven business trips, including four international trips lasting seven days each. I took a total of two road trips and twenty-two flights, including four transatlantic flights. I became an expert on the TSA regulations regarding breast milk. I often had to remind TSA agents of those rules.

I was subjected to every level of scrutiny, just short of a full strip search. I had my bags searched, my pump practically disassembled, and my ice packs swabbed. I was pulled out of line for pat downs on more than one occasion.

I was unfailingly polite and courteous. I understood why a little black bag with a motor, cords, and tubes might look suspicious. I made sure every agent between the ticket counter and x-ray machine knew I was packing, and I did everything possible to make it easy for security.

Maybe I should have worn a sign around my neck, translated into the local language, just so there was no confusion:

Milk for the baby
Lait pour le bébé
Leche para el bebé
Milch für das Baby
婴儿牛奶
赤ちゃんのためのミルク

I'll never forget a trip home from Germany. Not understanding the word pump, the security agents opened my pump, pulled out the breast cups, and then loudly exclaimed, while making melon-squeezing gestures with their hands, "Ohhh, for the baby!"

Ja, für das baby! That was just to get to my departure gate! I endured a multitude of other unpleasant experiences on my travels. I pumped in airport bathrooms, disgusted by the millions of germs swirling around me, but still mournful when I poured my milk down the sink. I pumped in airplane bathrooms; perched on top of the toilet seat, trying not to touch anything,

and praying we wouldn't hit turbulence.

I sat on the floor of conference rooms, lights off, huddled over my pump with my back to the door so no one could look in and see what I was doing. I pumped in closet-sized offices, kitchens, and locker rooms. Oh, the glamour of business travel as a pumping mom!

Fast forward to that fateful morning in 2012.

It was my first trip away from my youngest, and I was finally on my way home. I'd spent a week at a print shop in Quebec, up at all hours of the night to inspect and approve a catalog, while faithfully pumping every four hours to keep my supply up.

By the time I got to my hotel on Friday, I was absolutely exhausted. I had a 6:30 a.m. flight the next morning, so I asked for a 4:00 a.m. wake-up call. I needed enough time to pump before I checked out and drove to the airport.

I also asked if there was somewhere I could store my gigantic tote bag of frozen milk. The itty bitty freezer in my room wasn't going to cut it.

"No problem," the receptionist told me with a smile. "We'll put it in the freezer right behind the front desk."

I left my massive bag of liquid gold and retired to my room. The next morning I dragged my tired body to the front desk.

I was already cutting it close. Technically I should have been at the airport two hours before my international flight, but because the airport in Quebec City is tiny, I figured I'd be fine as long as I arrived by 5:00 a.m.

I turned in my keys, got my receipt, and asked for my milk. It was a different woman from the night before, so I had to explain the situation. She disappeared through the door and came back empty handed.

"There is no bag in the freezer," she told me.

As soon as the message reached my sleepy brain, my synapses snapped to attention and I was wide awake.

"What do you mean there's no bag in the freezer?" I asked politely, trying not to panic right away. "I left the bag last night when I checked in. There should be a message on my account."

"I'm sorry, Madame Goodman, there is no message."

"Would you please check again?" I asked.

She disappeared through the door again. After what felt like a lifetime, she returned, once again empty handed.

Now I was starting to freak out. I was going to miss my flight if I didn't leave for the airport soon, but there was no way I was leaving behind a week's worth of milk.

"C'est lait pour mon bébé. Où est-il? Où est-il?!"

I'm not sure why I thought shrieking hysterically in French would help matters, but I did it anyway. She must have sensed the impending meltdown in my shaky voice, blinking eyes, and crimson-colored face because she picked up the phone and called the manager.

A few more minutes ticked by, and I felt like I was going to be sick. Then another hotel employee burst through another door, triumphantly holding my bag. It had been moved to the large freezer in the kitchen.

Relief flooded my body, and I greedily snatched the precious parcel and clutched it to my body.

"Merci beaucoup! Merci beaucoup!" I shouted over my shoulder, as I gathered my luggage and rushed to my rental car.

As I peeled out of the parking lot and raced to the airport, my blood pressure dropped, and my pulse stopped reverberating in my ears. By the time I got to security, I had fully recovered. Disaster averted, or so I thought!

I greeted the first security agent with my passport in hand and a smile on my face. I even attempted to exchange pleasantries in French.

"Bonjour, ça va?"

Hello, how are you?

"Oui, ça va bien, mais je suis tres fatigue!"

Yes, it's going well, but I'm very tired.

I proceeded to the line and started to place my pump and milk on the conveyor belt. The next security agent approached

me, and I explained that I was traveling with a breast pump. He took a quick look at the pump and then zeroed in on the milk.

"Where is your baby?" he asked.

"I'm not traveling with my baby," I explained.

"Then you can't take this milk with you," he said.

Are you [insert expletive here, here, and here] kidding me?

This time I didn't panic. No, this time I was literally seeing red. Make that white. Blinding, hot, white rage was coursing through my veins.

You know how some people get really calm and quiet when they're angry, and it's scarier than any screaming, crying outburst?

I was one scary lady.

Through gritted teeth, I asked for the supervisor.

The poor man must have sensed my anger because he immediately summoned his supervisor, who quickly reassured me I could indeed take my milk home.

The rest of my trip was a blur. The security agent in Toronto completely ignored my milk but wasn't satisfied until he'd pawed through my pump, inspecting every inch of the bag. Then I couldn't find a place to pump until I walked to the other end of the terminal and found an empty family bathroom.

I locked the door, spread my coat on the floor, sat down, and started pumping. With no fear of TSA locking me away for going postal on the next agent who even looked at my milk, I started laughing uncontrollably at the absurdity of it all. I laughed so hard tears were streaming down my face.

Two more flights and a ninety-minute drive later, I pulled into my driveway. My husband and girls were waiting for me on the front porch. My oldest ran to me, and I scooped her up in my arms. Then I grabbed my baby and pulled her close, breathing in her sweet scent.

Cue the waterworks. Happy tears this time. I was home, and every horrible minute pumping, every frustrating security procedure, and every milk meltdown was worth this sweet reunion.

My nursing and pumping days are behind me now, but I'll never forget them. And now I've got written proof of all of the things I endured for my girls. Perfect for quelling their meltdowns in a few years!

"Honey, why are you so upset? Remember the time I schlepped breast milk all the way from Canada for you?"

Game over. I win.

Nicole Goodman is a full-time WAHM of two and the caffeine-driven mind behind Work in Sweats Mama. By day she joins the ranks of corporate America as a marketing specialist from the comfort of her home. Her commute consists of a quick descent down the stairs and a hard right into her office. She really does work in her sweats most days! After business hours, you'll find her chasing her fearless eighteen-month-old, verbally sparring with her precocious four-year-old, avoiding housework, and seeking an endorphin high on long runs. Nicole's idea of a fabulous vacation involves lots of GORP (Good Old Raisins and Peanuts) while backpacking in the National Park system, although trail running and stand-up paddle boarding in Hawaii are close seconds. She writes about motherhood, running, travel, and her obsession with athletic apparel and Fountain Coke at Work in Sweats Mama.

Welcome to Lego Stress Land

By Norine Dworkin-McDaniel
Science of Parenthood

Thus far, I regret breaking three things in my lifetime. More will surely come, but here's where the list stands at this point:

*Willard Woodrow's heart in the fourth grade.

*My dad's Alpha Romeo convertible sports car, crumpled nearly beyond repair in high school.

*The Lego model of the Hyena Droid Bomber from *Star Wars* that my five-year-old spent an entire afternoon building.

Guess which thing haunts me to this day?

The $30 pile of plastic, of course.

Star Wars junkie, um … devotee that he is, my kid had just started tinkering with bigger models. And with 232 pieces, the Hyena Droid Bomber was the most complex project he'd tackled yet. I'd pulled him away, reluctantly … briefly … for dinner. But after he'd gulped down his chicken and broccoli, he was back at work. He wanted to finish the model before bed. Just a few more steps and he'd be done.

Then I picked it up. Why? Why? Why? OH, WHY ON EARTH WOULD I PICK IT UP? I still ask myself that. I should have known better than to touch it; in the same way that promiscuous teens in horror movies should know better than to go wandering into creepy houses at night alone. But I'd wanted to take a closer look; to admire my son's handiwork. And, of course, you can see where this is going.

Almost instantly, a piece fell out of the middle. *Oops.* I tried shoving it back. It wouldn't connect. *That wasn't good.* I tried to force it into place. No go. *Crap. It fit before, why wouldn't it fit now?* As I struggled, more pieces came off in my hands. *Shit! Oh, this really, really wasn't good.* I started to panic as Fletcher, suddenly at my side, realized his once-whole bomber was falling to pieces in my hands.

"Fix it, Mommy! Fix it!" Fletcher hopped up and down beside me, visibly upset.

"I'm trying!" I growled. I could feel a headache starting at the base of my skull.

"Maaah-meeee!" my boy whined.

Now I was getting really annoyed. It's my least attractive quality—being easily angered when frustrated—especially when I created the frustrating situation myself. How did the fucking pieces go together? I frantically flipped back through the instruction booklet's assembly diagrams, trying to guess where to even start. Fletcher glared at me, angry tears filling his eyes. The model lay in chunks on the table. Somehow, in my hands, a whole day's efforts had come apart in under thirty seconds. And I didn't have a fucking clue how to put the thing back together again.

"YOU DESTROYED IT!" Fletcher turned on me with all the wounded fury of a five year old, grievously wronged.

"Do you know where these pieces go?" I demanded, my anger—at the Legos, at myself for breaking the Legos—about to boil over.

Fletcher shook his head furiously.

And then I lost it.

"WELL, NEITHER DO I!"

Welcome to what my friend Claudia calls Lego Stress Land. She has her own *Star Wars* Legos-obsessed son, so she's been here many times herself. It's the stationary equivalent of road rage, prompted not by idiot drivers but incomprehensible assembly

diagrams … and the infuriating realization that the pieces won't fit together nicely on Step 199 because your kid used the wrong piece all the way back on Step 8. It's the Murphy's Law of Lego building and you will only realize this grave, grave error when your child is *this close* to finishing. Then you'll have to undo hours of work, backtracking until you discover the mistake, and start over from there. It's enough to make you momentarily lose your grasp on reason and logic—not to mention impulse control—and start screaming like a lunatic. I believe the *DSM-V* describes this particular condition as Traumatic Lego Distress Disorder. If you've got a small boy and a short fuse, you know exactly what I'm talking about.

"Tearing the whole blessed thing apart makes me go crazy," Claudia admitted to me when we compared Lego horror stories one day over sushi. "We've gotten to the point where my son crashes the whole thing on the floor."

Amazing, isn't it, that colored plastic can engender such fury? The Lego folks should seriously consider getting into the anger management market. If you can build a Lego model with 400-plus pieces without losing your cool and taking a meat cleaver to the entire project, congratulations. You could be the next Dalai Lama. Actually, the Dalai Lama is probably the only one who should be allowed to build Legos. The rest of us are just ticking time bombs.

And yes, folks, it takes one time bomb with a super-short fuse to know one. I had been dreading the day I'd be called upon to play Legos ever since the maternal-fetal tech had spotted my son's penis on the ultrasound, confirming I was having a boy. I didn't grow up playing with Legos. There were no Lego Friends sets back then. I played Barbie, house, and had tea parties. Girly-girl that I'd been, I was nervous enough about being able to play boy games with my son. But of all of the boy toys that I knew were in my future after the ultrasound tech gleefully announced, "It's a boy!"—the Ninja Turtles, the Power Rangers, the Transformers—it was the Legos that filled my new mom's heart with particular dread.

I'd had a couple of years to observe my nephews' Lego phases; the way they'd sit for hours at their kitchen table, utterly absorbed by their models, deaf to everything but the click of plastic on plastic. When I peeked over their shoulders, the instruction diagrams seemed so dizzyingly complex; I was completely intimidated. There was no way I'd be able to negotiate that! But of course, I tried. Fletcher loved building towers with the big, clunky baby Legos. When he could finally start doing more complicated kits like his cousins, he was beyond thrilled. For one ridiculously naïve moment, I thought, maybe we'll have fun doing this together after all!

As it turned out, I was a terrible person to build Lego models with. I'd start hyperventilating if those cellophane bags of Lego bits got opened on the living room coffee table. The table's wide wood slats had gaps between them that were like magnets to itty-bitty Lego pieces. The pieces were practically guaranteed to fall through and be lost forever, prompting many tears (mostly mine) when the model I'd spent $38 bucks on couldn't be finished because the parts had gone missing. But what really punched my buttons—and I mean really made me crazy— was not sorting the pieces by color, *as every instruction booklet recommends*. Fletcher loved to just start slapping pieces together willy-nilly, then whine that he couldn't find the one tiny, light gray rectangle block buried beneath the heap of other plastic pieces. One afternoon, I came absolutely unglued trying to piece together a simple helicopter kit meant for six-year-olds. At that point, my cooler-headed husband, who designs and builds water filtration systems for public aquariums—which are kinda like real-life Legos, when you think about it—made an executive decision. From then on, *he* would be in charge of Lego building. Better for my blood pressure if I stuck with bedtime stories and board games, Stewart reasoned. Fine by me. I rock at Candyland.

But back to the bomber model scattered all over the kitchen table and my distraught child sobbing into the couch cushions …

Stewart was away on a business trip, so it was up to me to make things right. I couldn't stand seeing my child miserable because something he'd invested time and effort in had broken. Correction: Something *I'd* broken. So, I poured myself a very large martini and surveyed the damage. *You can do this*, I pep-talked myself. *Slow and steady. It's not that hard. Kids make these things all the time. Kids also program digital video recorders,* I reminded myself, *and I haven't figured out that trick yet either.* But this was more important than being able to watch *Will & Grace* reruns. So I methodically worked my way back through the diagrams, removing piece after piece until I discovered where the errant part actually belonged. It clicked smoothly into place.

Over the next hour—and yet another jumbo martini—I carefully rebuilt the bomber to the point where it had fallen apart. Now Fletcher could pick up where he'd left off. He'd finish the model in no time.

"Look," I said to Fletcher, still buried in the couch cushions. He shook his head, refusing to even turn around. "C'mon, look what Mommy did." Slowly, I coaxed Fletcher to turn his teary face to me and held up the reassembled model. "See? Mommy fixed it."

"Let me see," he said, not quite believing. Then … a huge smile.

I know I won't be able to handle every setback or disappointment Fletcher experiences, but in that moment, managing the plastic ones felt like a victory for both of us.

Norine Dworkin-McDaniel created Science of Parenthood and serves as its Chief of Scientific Snarkiness. When she's not blogging about the endless mysteries of parenting a seven-year-old at Don't Put Lizards In Your Ears and Lifescript's Parent Talk blog, she works as a freelance writer. Her articles have appeared in More, Health, Parents, American Baby, Redbook, Marie Claire, Shape, iVillage, All You, and Prevention. She's currently finishing a memoir about being a late-in-life mom.

BONUS #3

Rock You Like a Hurricane
By Nicole Goodman

*I*n Mayan legend, the storm god Hurakan ruled the large winds and evil spirits. Once a year, Mayans sacrificed a young woman to appease Hurakan. She was tossed into the sea, along with a warrior to guide her to Hurakan's underwater kingdom.

In Greek mythology, Aeolus, the ruler of the winds, kept the twelve winds in a cave with a dozen holes, all blocked by stones. When he wanted the wind to blow from a certain direction, Aeolus rolled away a stone. When he opened all twelve holes, he unleashed a hurricane.

In modern folklore, we have the indomitable force of nature known simply as Mother.

She can rock you like a hurricane. Building strength and speed over time, Mom can unleash a storm of epic proportions, also known as the mother of all meltdowns.

Before it reaches full-blown disaster status, a meltdown must progress through four distinct stages: 1) Disturbance—A discrete event originates and remains intact for a sustained period of time; 2) Depression—The disturbance develops a closed circulation, swirling around a central point of pressure; 3) Storm—Intensity and power increase, and the meltdown is given a name; and 4) Meltdown—Now at full strength, the meltdown is categorized on a scale of one to five based on potential for destruction.

Mommy Meltdown Scale

All meltdowns are scary, but some have the potential for real danger. The combination of speed, surge, strength, and other factors determine the meltdown's destructive power. To help those within the storm's path better prepare, forecasters use a disaster-potential scale which assigns meltdowns to five categories:

Category 1: Minimal damage. No real damage to buildings or permanent structures. Damage primarily to unanchored household items, such as lamps, dishes, or discarded toys.

Category 2: Moderate damage. Damage to peripheral materials, such as framed art, knick-knacks, and chotskies. Considerable damage to vegetation and furniture. Secondary escape routes blocked.

Category 3: Extensive damage. Some structural damage to small buildings, including doll dwellings, forts, and play houses. Larger structures damaged by storm debris.

Category 4: Extreme damage. Complete structural failure, including shattered windows and mirrors, kicked-in doors, and fist-sized holes in drywall. Primary escape routes treacherous.

Category 5: Catastrophic. Evacuate immediately.

Early Warning Signs

Modern technology provides numerous ways to detect and track meltdowns. If you don't have access to advanced warning systems, look for these early warning signs:

Increased Swell, Decreased Period Between Surges—As a storm approaches, swells in temper and irritability will increase in size, while the period between surges will decrease. Eventually, choppy retorts and tears will take over.

Falling Barometer—As the meltdown gets closer, you'll notice a significant drop in pressure. This eerie lull in tension is just the calm before the storm.

Marked Increase in Speed—By the time you notice the whirlwind of motion and commotion, Mom is well on her way to full meltdown status. The storm will make landfall soon.

Squalls—The outer bands of the storm can arrive well before the full force of the meltdown hits home. Don't wait until it's too late. Seek shelter immediately.

Be Prepared

Heed the warnings and steer clear of the storm. No matter where the meltdown falls on the scale, it's best to err on the side of caution and be prepared for the worst.

Follow these helpful hints to minimize damage:

Before the Storm
- Make a communication plan. Know how to get in touch with emergency contacts (Dad, Grandma, Mom's Bestie, Mom's Masseuse) at all times.
- Identify potential hazards and secure your property. Remove all unanchored items from the storm's path.
- Learn evacuation routes. Arrange transportation if necessary.
- Consider a safe room. Check Dad's man cave in the basement or garage for storm-readiness.

During the Storm
- Follow all instructions from officials (Dad, Grandma).
- Evacuate, if necessary.
- If you are unable to evacuate, take refuge in a small room, closet, or hallway.
- Stay away from glass windows and doors.
- Don't be fooled by the relative calm at the eye of the storm. The final wallop will follow.

After the Storm
- Stay alert and tread carefully.
- If evacuated, return home only when officials (Dad, Grandma) say it's safe.
- Give Mom a big hug and offer to clean up.

Storms can be scary, but they're just nature's way of letting off steam. Remember, after the storm comes the rainbow.

And, don't worry, sacrificing young maidens and warriors is outdated. But bribes involving chocolate, shoes, and long, uninterrupted showers may appease the storm goddess and prevent Mom's next meltdown!

Be Right Back, Mommy's Having a Meltdown

By Karen Blessing
Baking In A Tornado

I'm not really one to have a meltdown. I'm more the "go and hide" type. I may feel sorry for myself, even shed a tear or two, but meltdowns really aren't my style.

And then I had teenagers. I really didn't mean to; I meant to have babies. Somewhere along the line that whole "having cute babies" thing came back to bite me on the A$$, and there were teenagers living right there in my home.

The one time I did have a meltdown, it started with a bad choice made by a middle-schooler. It could have ended there. It should have ended there.

I had been a SAHM, but when my kids were in the 7th and 8th grades I decided to get a part-time job. I left after them in the morning and got home just an hour after they did in the afternoon. There were a few things going on that I didn't like; rules being broken in that hour before I got home, but nothing life threatening.

One day I came home to find muddy footprints on my cream-colored, carpeted stairway all the way to my son's room, where the screen was out of the window. Don't ask. I didn't.

Friends were not allowed in the house when I wasn't home, but another day I found out that my boys (and apparently half the neighborhood) were coming into the house, going out onto the back deck, and jumping down onto the lawn. *Can you say law suit?* Fortunately, I didn't have to.

And although kids aren't supposed to be drinking soda in my living room, I came home one day to find the carpet soaked with something sticky and sweet smelling. I never did find out what it was since it appears that no one knew a single thing about it.

So discussions were had and consequences were spelled out and we did settle into a routine.

Until that fateful day …

I was at work when the school principal called my cell. He started by telling me that there had been a fight and my heart sank. My kids were not raised to be fighters. Sneaky rule breakers apparently, but not fighters.

It turns out that I was right. They weren't fighters. It also turns out that the fight took place after school and just outside of the school grounds. Someone who saw it went to the principal and he was looking into it. And the principal was informed that my Older-Son-Who-Shall-Remain-Nameless (OS, for short) was not only there, but had videotaped it on his phone. The principal wanted that video.

Once I got my jaw to close again, I quit my job and headed home to talk to OS.

When I got home, I found out that one of the kids involved in the fight was a good friend of my son. I found something else out as well. While I was driving home, this friend's mother called OS and ordered him to delete the video.

OS could have gotten his friend into a lot of trouble. I was very conflicted about his friend's mother; partially furious and partially relieved that she had called my son behind my back. I was uncomfortable with the position the principal had put us into as well, expecting us to turn over video of an incident that didn't take place at the school and could ultimately result in OS getting some of his classmates in trouble. I was now faced with having to tell the principal what he wasn't going to want to hear

… that the video was gone. I was also dealing with the second kid's mom who called the house wanting my assurance that the fight wouldn't end up on YouTube. This had turned into a full-fledged cluster-cluck.

There was also the rather huge issue of OS's judgment to be addressed. My son claimed that the fight didn't start out as real, but as staged. It didn't matter. He used poor judgment, and as bad as it was, this could have ended up even worse. When there's a fight, you get help. Period. Videoing is not an option.

This incident was the topic of conversation, and by that I mean many, many conversations. The repercussions of OS's poor choice seemed to be never-ending. But he was young, and I figured between seeing the fallout, realizing the huge issue this had become and how much worse it could have been, and losing his phone for a week, we'd just call it "lesson learned." If in the future he took the time to think situations through more carefully, well, that's what parenting is about. You take these opportunities to make an impression and help your child to mature.

Wouldn't it be great if this were the end of the story? No such luck.

The next year my son moved on to high school, and at the beginning of the school year there was a fight in the main lobby.

Guess what my son did?

Feel it coming? Meltdown on the way? Wait, you haven't heard the best part …

There was no call from the school this time. OS told me about it himself. Showed me the video on his phone, in fact. Because just doing the opposite of what I say is not enough for this teenager. Certainly not. *Where's the fun if he doesn't really get in there and rub my nose in it?*

Is it getting hot in here? That would be my blood pressure rising so high it's actually heating up the earth. *Global warming?* I may have to own that.

Meltdown? Hell yeah. I lost it—honestly and truly, fully, and thoroughly. There was screaming and punishing and taking away of multiple belongings. There was grounding and ranting and pacing and oblivion to the fact that all the windows were open and all the neighbors could hear.

Then, too embarrassed to face those neighbors after my meltdown, we may or may not have put our house on the market.

I really do love my new home. Unfortunately it's only a few miles from the last one so my son was able to find it.

It's four years later and he's in college now. I may or may not eventually give him his phone back. Probably not.

Karen Blessing, formerly a Director of Social Service and a Retail Buyer, is now a SAHM to two teens. She's still serving and buying, just with the money going out instead of coming in. She started baking to feed the hordes of teens who've made her basement their home, and continued when she realized it relieves stress. Finding herself with more stress than butter and sugar, she blogs, shares recipes, and vents at Baking In A Tornado. Karen's been featured on the websites Mamapedia, Scary Mommy, GenerationFabulous, and Treat a Day and is published in the Life Well Blogged series of books.

Take Two Meltdowns and Call Me in the Morning

By Michelle Nahom
A Dish of Daily Life

Let me preface this story by saying I have nothing but respect for the medical profession. But when one of my children had a serious medical condition, I had a few encounters with doctors who treated me as if my concerns were unimportant. A meltdown was almost inevitable. I don't often lose my cool, at least in front of people I don't know well, but *this* was one of those occasions.

Let me start from the beginning ...

The day that my world turned upside down started out like any other day. My preschool-age daughter had a friend over, and they were eating macaroni and cheese on the back porch. My youngest son, who was a little over one at the time, had eaten his lunch inside in the kitchen, where I was, and was just kind of toddling around the room. And then all of the sudden, he wasn't toddling around the room. He was on the floor, turning blue, and foaming at the mouth. His eyes rolled back; I thought he was choking. He passed out. Everything I learned in infant CPR slipped away. I had NO idea what to do. Panicked, I called 911. Fortunately he started breathing again on his own before the paramedics arrived, since it took them forever! Actually, it was only fifteen or twenty minutes, but when something like this happens, every minute seems like an eternity. So, he wasn't choking after all. But the paramedics had no idea what had happened so they wanted to transport him to the hospital. My husband couldn't understand why I hadn't just put our son in the car and run to the hospital myself, since it's literally five minutes from our house. But it's hard to explain how paralyzed I was. I was in panic mode. I couldn't think. I couldn't act.

Honestly, the rest of that first day was a blur. I don't remember much other than the picture of him I have in my mind, lying on the ground, turning blue. That image will be imprinted in my mind forever.

At the hospital, the doctors were unable to tell us what had happened. But after that day, these episodes, which looked like seizures, began to happen on a regular basis. It was like there was life before and life after he got sick. Life after was very different from life before. These episodes weren't happening daily, but they *were* frequent. And they would hit with no warning! My son would turn white as a ghost, and then he'd just stop breathing, turn blue, and pass out. I was a wreck. Every time it happened, I thought we were going to lose him. We were constantly fearful, constantly on edge. But we tried to keep as much normalcy in our lives as possible as the doctors ran tests, and he spent time in and out of hospitals.

During this time, my son's pediatrician also caught a problem with his blood cell production, and the word leukemia was mentioned. As I write this, I'm reliving all those emotions. My heart just dropped. Hearing those words is a parent's worst nightmare. I can't remember what the condition actually was, but I remember specialists telling us it was rare, and they thought it might have been a reaction to some sort of virus, but they really didn't know. He ended up having to have a blood transfusion. Had he not started producing those blood cells again, he would have had to continue having the transfusions until he did.

Meanwhile, he continued to have the episodes that looked like seizures. One day when he hadn't had one in a few days,

we decided to go to a nearby lake with friends. We should have known better. It happened again, and we were nowhere near a hospital. Someone on the beach with a cell phone handy called 911, and off my son went in an ambulance for a second time. The ER doctor that saw him suggested to me that he was throwing temper tantrums—holding his breath and that was why he was passing out.

I HAD TO RESTRAIN MYSELF.

I honestly wanted to slap that doctor. But I didn't. I had to force myself to take some deep breaths and let it go. I knew my own kid, and I knew this wasn't caused by temper tantrums. But this probably set the stage for my first meltdown.

My son was released from the hospital later in the afternoon. I had originally made plans to go to my dinner club that night, but I hadn't made my dish and, honestly, I was drained from the events of the day. My husband convinced me to go anyway; he thought I needed a break. At this point, these passing-out episodes had been going on for a while, and both my husband and I were a mess. We weren't sleeping at night, for fear our son would stop breathing, and we were completely stressed by the fact that the doctors just couldn't figure out why this was happening! Of course, you know what I am going to say, *don't you?* Just as I was getting ready to leave, it happened again. He stopped breathing and passed out, for the second time that day. We got in the car and drove with him to the hospital.

To me, twice in one day was cause for even more panic. It had never happened twice in one day before, and my worry was that the problem was going to start escalating. Our second ER doctor of the day basically brushed it off, telling me that he wouldn't be able to call our pediatrician because another group of doctors that they switched off with was on call instead. I think I was fairly polite when I told him that he needed to call our pediatrician anyway because this was an ongoing problem, and the other physician's group wasn't aware of my son's condition.

He then let me know if our physician's group wasn't on call, he couldn't disturb them, because they would get mad. He tried to tell me if they did that for everyone, then the doctors would never get a break.

And you know what? He was right. I respect their right to have a break. I get it. I do. But when you're feeling like I was feeling right then and there, when you're worrying that each time your child turns blue it might be the last time, you don't exactly think properly. In my mind, my doctor's BREAK was a lot less important to me than my child's LIFE!

I COMPLETELY LOST IT.

I yelled at that doctor. I told him if my child died because he didn't want to call our pediatrician because he might get mad, it was going to be on his head. I don't really remember what else I said, but I was not nice.

I HAD A SERIOUS MELTDOWN.

I'm not proud of myself for losing it, but every time this happened, I didn't know if my son would start breathing again. Every time he turned blue, I wondered if it would be the last time. I was scared for my baby.

Needless to say, that ER doctor (or maybe it was the on-call doctor) did call my son's pediatrician after my little tirade, and he was not mad. He was worried. He wanted our son transferred to another hospital immediately for more testing. We spent the night in a children's hospital in another town.

My second meltdown happened because of a (supposedly) highly-regarded children's neurologist. She had scheduled a test for my son; a test that we had to wait a month for and during this time, there were no changes in his condition. He continued to stop breathing, turn blue, and pass out on a regular basis. Keep in mind that all of this was very well documented at this point. It had been going on for months.

The procedure was scheduled for a Monday, and on the Friday before, we received a call from the hospital asking routine questions. One of the questions was, "Does he ever stop breathing suddenly?" Hello … this was what the problem was! So of course I said, "Yes." The person who called then told me he couldn't have this particular procedure because of that. She told me she was sorry, but they'd have to reschedule. When I asked her how long that would take, she told me she didn't know, but it could be several weeks to a month. We'd already waited a month at this point, and this was their mistake, not ours! So I called my pediatrician and left a message. When he called me back, he reassured me and told me to call the neurologist's office right away, that she'd be able to handle this. She was aware of his condition, as we'd met with her a number of times, and she seemed nice enough. Unfortunately, at this point it was after five, but my pediatrician said to call her anyway, because he wanted to make sure we kept the procedure on the schedule for Monday.

So I called. And she SCREAMED at me. She said things like, "how dare I call her after five," "the procedure will just have to rescheduled," and "it wasn't her problem." I was SHAKING because she was so nasty to me. This was my child's life we were talking about, and she yelled me at me because I called a little after five on a Friday! I apologized for calling her, although I should have just hung up. Then I called my pediatrician back. I didn't yell at anyone, but I might have been a tad bit hysterical. I told him what had happened. He was stunned. I told him I wanted another neurologist because there was no way that woman was ever going near my son again. I believe my exact words to him were, "She doesn't care whether my son lives or dies, and I don't want her near him ever again!"

Maybe the neurologist had had a bad day. But if you're a pediatric neurologist, you need to have a little more empathy for a parent that is stressed because her child stops breathing and turns blue on a regular basis. You need to figure out a solution when it's your office staff's incompetence (or maybe it was the hospital) that made a mistake on the procedure, because his condition was well documented in all of his records. Not to mention you had several conversations with us, the parents. And, no matter what, you don't scream at a stressed-out mom.

In the end, the seizure-like episodes stopped when we discovered my son had food allergies. None of the doctors would say that was the final diagnosis, but after we took him to the allergist and eliminated wheat from his diet, it never happened again. He was on a wheat-free diet for two years before we found out he had outgrown the allergy.

I am thankful to our pediatrician and his office staff for getting us through a really rough time. I am thankful that it wasn't more serious than it was. And more than anything, I am thankful for the gift of life. This difficult time in our lives gave me a new respect for how precious life really is.

Michelle Nahom is a mom of three and a serial entrepreneur. She spends her time running her kids all over for various sports, trying to figure out what to make for dinner at the last minute, and fighting a never-ending battle with clutter (and her kids' rooms). She loves photography, social media, running, and, of course, her family (including three dogs and four cats)! Visit her at her blog, A Dish of Daily Life.

It's Getting Hot in Here

By Janine Huldie
Janine's Confessions of a Mommyaholic

Nowadays, it takes a lot for me to lose my cool. I'm the mom of two little girls who are sixteen months apart; my oldest just turned four years old and my youngest will be three by the end of the year. I have seen and done it all in the time I have been their mother. I have dealt with colic, lactose and soy allergies, formula feedings (because the same baby wouldn't latch), hypoallergenic formulas …

Then it was onto to teething, the terrible twos, potty-training … rinse and repeat with baby number two! For most of this time, if not all of it, I have held myself together.

In my younger years, however, I could fly off the handle very easily—rivaling a truck driver or sailor with my mouth! Hell, my grandfather, who was in the army during WWII, told me this on more than one occasion when I was a teen. To be quite honest, it made me feel special that, in his eyes, he considered me to be like him, because he truly was a hero and I grew up adoring and idolizing him.

Many years have lapsed though—that was then and this is now. To be fair, he has been gone since Valentine's Day 1999 and it is now summer 2013—a mere fourteen years and various changes later. I am now not only a grown up by all accounts, but have major life responsibilities, including a family to take care of and support. Which brings me to my meltdown …

On this very day in question it was the middle of July, and we were inside of major a heat wave. Heading for over 100 degrees, it felt as though someone had opened the door to the oven in our home.

Our central air conditioning unit stopped working the night before. Yes, it was seriously perfect timing (not!) and yes, before you ask, calls were indeed made to our usual air conditioning guy. Unfortunately, we didn't hear right back from him. While waiting, we called a few others. One had the audacity to quote us twice the price to fix the problem and could, of course, fix it the same day.

We may have been hot and miserable, but we were not about to be taken for fools. Having been a business major (undergraduate work), I understand the dynamics of supply and demand. Trust me, you take enough economics classes and the concept doesn't escape. It was hot, but not hot enough that we were going to let this guy rip us off or jip us!

After what seemed like an eternity, our regular guy called and told us he would squeeze us in that same day. In the meantime, I had spent the morning with fans running and windows open hoping against hope that something would indeed make a difference.

It was now around 1:00 p.m. My kids had eaten both breakfast and lunch, while I worked on catching up on blogging. Alright, so I may have slightly lost track of time and yes, they were oh so quiet while I was busy reading and writing. This should have been my first clue that something was indeed amiss. Seriously, nine times out of ten no good comes from quiet children!

When I finally finished and turned around, I found toys everywhere and the new PLAY-DOH my oldest had just received from her grandmother broken into small pieces all over the floor, under her craft table, and ground into our living room carpet.

I would never have gotten her PLAY-DOH for her birthday, but my husband decided to tell his mom this would be a great gift for her, because she loves playing with it at school. Now, I

know why it stays at school. The mess that I incurred from this harmless crafting toy was nothing short of horrendous.

As I surveyed the damage, I felt my blood boiling, matching my overheated body temperature. If I were an old-time cartoon character like Bugs Bunny from the Looney Tunes, steam would have been rising, rushing, and gushing from my ears. You would have also heard loud horns to match my level of anger.

And then it happened. I completely lost it and screamed like the *sun wasn't coming out tomorrow*. Sorry, Annie, but this was just how I felt! I saw this movie as a child, but I had no idea until that moment why the sun can't always come out the next day!

In the moments that followed, I loudly and boldly told my girls that they needed to get out of the play area and go sit on their beds while mommy vacuumed. I also let them know in between my loud yelling just how annoyed and ticked off I was. I might even have said that they were so very bad for doing this and asked over and over again how they could make a mess like this in only an hour's time.

In the meantime, I starting vacuuming and swearing to God. As I was doing this, the girls were sitting in timeout on their beds. It's possible they heard everything escaping my mouth— that young girl whose grandfather would have been proud by the language she was spilling had returned. I released a good many obscenities that I had bottled up for years.

In between vacuuming, I was forced onto my hands and knees to pick up ground-in PLAY-DOH, all the while seething. The entire event was one gigantic PLAY-DOH nightmare!

While on the ground simmering, I had sweat pouring out of me from places I didn't even know existed. And I'd released so much of my anger and frustrations on the vacuum, the poor Dyson appeared to be quivering; most likely wondering, *what next*?

Once I was done vacuuming, I felt so much better. It was as if some huge load had been lifted from my shoulders. As crazy as it sounds, I wasn't annoyed anymore. I was now disgustingly grimy and feeling quite gross from the sweating that had just occurred.

But guess what?

After my mommy meltdown, I discovered my two PLAY-DOH demons sound asleep! The white noise of the vacuum had knocked them out, and they were sleeping like angels. The last time a vacuum put anyone to sleep it was my colicky baby. Ironically that baby was now my four-year-old and the one who had the PLAY-DOH that started this whole mess. That is how we ended up needing a new vacuum the first time around. We all fell asleep that night waiting for her to drift off. You can say the vacuum has healing powers around these parts, for sure, but we do end up giving these gems a good workout in the process!

With the mess being cleaned up and kids sleeping, I actually got to take a nice cold shower to get off the sweaty, dirty grossness. And I can say that a cold shower never felt better! Since they were sleeping, I actually enjoyed bathing for once, instead of worrying the entire time about how long I was taking.

You might be wondering at this point if our air conditioning ever got fixed. The answer is … yes! The air conditioning was fixed later that night and to top it off we got to go to Friendly's to cool off for dinner and ice cream. Dinner would, of course, be interrupted with my oldest child needing to urgently use the bathroom as I tried to take the last bite of my meal. But that's a story for another day!

Maybe I should have more mommy meltdowns in the future. With rewards like long, cold showers and ice cream, those crazy episodes actually turn into mini-vacations!

Janine Huldie is a certified, licensed teacher who currently manages a home and family, all while trying to keep peace and balance with minimal meltdowns from all. She is a wife to Kevin and a mom to her two little girls, who are sixteen months apart. Her oldest, Emma, just turned four and her youngest, Lily, will be three years old in November. Her days are also filled with her love of writing and passion for design, too. You can find her at Janine's Confessions of a Mommyaholic and J9 Designs.

A Dresser Full

By Ginny Marie
Lemon Drop Pie

From the first time I saw her, I knew she was different from her sister. This was a surprise to me. *How could a newborn show so much personality from the moment of birth?*

My oldest daughter, Lily, would nurse through any situation and contentedly fall asleep at my breast. Emmy, on the other hand, was not so easily subdued. I spent most of my first Mother's Day with Emmy in the back of my van nursing her where it was quiet, instead of eating dinner in the fancy restaurant with the rest of my family. She would push me away when she was satisfied and sleep only when she wanted to.

Despite her need for a quiet place to nurse, my youngest child could attract the attention of everyone in the room or on the street or in the grocery store with the noise of her tantrums. I would smile with embarrassment when Emmy was in the middle of one of these hair raising screams, telling those around me that she was okay ... really, she was just overreacting. I would act calm and collected on the outside, while I was a raving lunatic on the inside, wondering why my child would put me through such an ordeal.

Worst of all, when Emmy was in the middle of a fit, sometimes she would cry so hard she would throw up all over herself. I would beg her to calm down, as this was the child who gagged on anything. At my nephew's graduation ceremony, I tried to quiet her by feeding her a soft Gerber Star, since of course she wouldn't nurse. Instead, she gagged on it, throwing up all over herself and on my lap. I took her out of the auditorium in horror. Although I am usually a well-prepared mother, that day I hadn't thought to bring a change of clothes for the baby or for myself. I grabbed some baby wipes from the diaper bag and frantically wiped off my skirt and Emmy's little dress in the washroom before I snuck back in to the graduation, reeking of baby vomit.

As she grew older, Emmy would have fits if I didn't bring a snack on the five minute walk to pick up her sister from school or when it was time to leave the park. If I refused to buy that really cute stuffed kitten at the grocery store, she would burst in loud, sobbing tears. Once, my husband and I decided to take the girls to a restaurant. Almost as soon as we sat down in the crowded room, both girls decided to fuss. We left without even looking at the menu.

I was the mother who would walk away from her screaming child, hoping that she would follow me on her own. (She usually did.) I was the mother who smiled, face beet red, telling people who walked by staring at us that Emmy was fine, she was just upset. I'm also the mother who smiles when I'm shopping alone and hears someone else's child having a tantrum. When that happens, I thank God that my own drama llama is at home and not with me.

Now that Emmy is in Kindergarten, her temper tantrums have lessened. She is well-behaved at restaurants and doesn't cry when I say no at the store. She knows when it's time to leave the park. She doesn't scream on the sidewalk any more. However, there is one thing that she is very stubborn about. Getting dressed!

I started off the year feeling like a great mother. Every morning, I would lay her outfit on her bed, only to have Emmy reject the outfit I chose for her. Finally I got smart, or so I thought. I started leaving two outfits on her bed for her to choose from. Emmy would come downstairs wearing a completely different,

clashing outfit. "This is okay." I thought. "She's independent. This is good!" I stopped picking out her clothes and let her choose what she was going to wear.

Who cared if she wore a red shirt with purple leggings or that her favorite shirt was too small and showed her belly? I held my tongue and hid her favorite threadbare clothes.

But then I noticed a trend that I was not too happy about. Every day, I would walk into her room and discover that she had thrown her discarded choices from the dresser onto the floor. I would pick up her clothes that were still clean, fold them, and place them back into the correct drawer. I tried to guide her in the mornings and told her not to throw her clothes on the floor. I tried to have her pick out an outfit the night before. But every morning, Emmy rejected her earlier choice and changed her mind. She threw her neatly folded clothes all over the floor until she found something she wanted to wear. She would pull dresses off hangers and leave them in clumps until she found what she liked. Her hamper overflowed with clothes that had been worn for three days in a row or had been worn for only two minutes.

Her dresser got messier and messier as I lost patience and started to throw clothes back into her drawers every morning without taking the time to fold them again. I had places to go, work to do. I began getting frustrated with my daughter, who was not taking my loving advice, who was NOT cooperating in the wardrobe department. She wouldn't wear that shirt because the sequins itched, and she wouldn't wear those pants because the buttons had writing on them. It would be time to go to school and Emmy would barely be dressed.

Finally, one morning I walked into her room to "help" her pick out her clothes. It seemed like the entire contents of her dresser were already on the floor. I had to go to work that morning after dropping the kids off at school. I thought about the never-ending cycle of laundry; the overflowing hampers, the laundry baskets full of clean clothes waiting to be folded. Something rose up in me as I looked at Emmy's bedroom floor, at all those previously neatly folded clothes just lying there like casualties of the tornado that was Emmy. Then, I looked at my daughter. She was standing there, in her underwear, stubbornly refusing to get dressed because she couldn't find anything to wear in the piles surrounding her.

"If you don't want to wear any of these clothes," I said, "I'll give them to little girls who *will* wear them!" I scooped up an armful of clothes from her floor, carried them to my bedroom, and flung them on my floor.

"Mommy, wait!" cried Emmy. "I'll get dressed!"

"You have all these clothes that are practically brand new!" I was really getting into it. "Goodwill is going to love getting *all these clothes*!" I took a drawer out of Emmy's dresser and tossed the contents onto my already growing pile.

"No, Mommy, I'll wear them! I promise!" Emmy thought I had gone out of my mind. She wasn't far off. Another drawer found its way into my arms. More clothes landed on the pile.

"Some little girl who DOESN'T THROW HER CLOTHES ON THE FLOOR will love these!" I yelled through the doorway at my daughter.

"MOMMY, LOOK, I'M DRESSED!" Emmy said, tears rolling down her cheeks. In less than two minutes I had completely unraveled. The patient, independence-nurturing mother had completely turned all the dresser drawers completely upside down until not a single pair of fairy panties or ballet pink tights was left in her dresser. When we left the house that morning, Emmy's dresser and bedroom floor had been cleared out, and my bedroom floor was piled high with her clothes.

After school, Emmy and I went through the heap of clothes together. We sorted through the clothes that she wanted to keep and put them neatly into her dresser. The clothes that were too old or full of holes went into the garbage, and clothes that were too small or too itchy went into a bag for donation. I also kept one or two outfits aside for sentimental reasons.

I'd like to say that I've never lost my temper again and that Emmy has never thrown clothes on the floor either. You and I both know I'd be lying. I still yell and Emmy still misses the hamper. We sort through our piles filled with the weariness of mommyhood and stubbornness of a Kindergartener, and somehow we still end up with a dresser full of blessings.

Ginny Marie writes at Lemon Drop Pie about the joys of motherhood after breast cancer. Ginny was named a BlogHer Heart Voice of the Year in 2013. She enjoys nature and reading with her family. She does not enjoy temper tantrums or doing laundry. Fortunately, the dryer only had a temper tantrum once. Ginny promptly put the dryer in a time out and called the repairman.

Embracing the Meltdowns, Even the Ones about Poop

By Stephanie Farley
Crayon Marks and Tiger Stripes

Road trips. I used to love them. But now that I have a toddler, I sing a different song.

Before becoming a mother, road trips used to mean carrying on a conversation without interruptions, singing lovely duets with my husband, and sometimes just enjoying the quiet (I don't even remember what that sounds like anymore!). Now road trips consist of a loud DVD player, obnoxiously noisy iPad apps, a basketful of toys that takes up the entire back seat, frequent whining, and oh-so-many stops because who wants to sit in a car seat for thirteen or more hours?!

I live in the middle of nowhere—drought ridden, treeless West Texas. As bad as I make that sound, I have come to love the beauty of being able to see halfway across the earth, and the sunsets are amazing. I grew up where my parents live in the green, hilly, beautifulness of Missouri. So naturally, flat Texas took some getting used to. There are 850 miles between us and my parents, which is a 13-hour trek across the Midwest on a good day. With a toddler, you can go ahead and estimate that to be sixteen hours or more. That's sixteen hours of pure bliss.

And with a road trip that long, you can be sure there are going to be meltdowns.

As a mom, I have endured my fair share of meltdowns. Some leave me questioning my remaining sanity, some leave me feeling sympathetic, and some are just downright funny. This particular meltdown is very much the latter. It also happens to be my most embarrassing parenting moment … wait, scratch that. How about the most embarrassing moment of my life? Yeah, that sounds like a more accurate description.

It was one of those road trips that felt like eternity. "Are we there yet? Are we there yet? ARE WE THERE YET?" I'm pretty sure time slows down exponentially when you are in a car with a toddler.

In general, my handsome little red-headed boy, who we will lovingly refer to as E, has always been a very easy kid. He was sleeping through the night at eight weeks old. (Yes, I was the mom that woke up, realized that he had slept through the night, and ran to his crib convinced that I am either the deafest person on earth or that he was dead.) He is good at entertaining himself. He loves to do learning activities. He is very thoughtful. He's an extrovert (I wonder who he gets that from?) and doesn't know a stranger, which can be kind of scary at times. He doesn't have too many temper tantrums. But let me tell you that when he does, his red hair really shines through. Overall, he's a pretty easy kid.

Let me rephrase that. He *was* a pretty easy kid, until he turned two. Any mom that has survived the toddler years can relate. Any kid that is deemed "easy" loses that status when they hit two. There's the "Mine!" phase, the inability-to-share phase, the never-sitting-still phase, the motor-mouth phase, the "I DO IT!" phase, the wreck-the-house-in-every-way-possible phase, and the potty-training phase. Come to think of it, all of these phases seemed to hit us at once. Lord, have mercy!

On a road trip, we have a 50/50 chance of E behaving and being the best child ever or sprouting horns and doing his best impression of a demon. Luckily for us, this trip was a good one, at least until we stopped for a potty break. Then he quickly lost "best child ever" status.

We pulled into the gas station. With great enthusiasm, E exclaimed, "We go eat in there! Eat in there!"

I swear he has been going through a growth spurt since he hit two years old. Eating has become his favorite pastime. I fear for my checkbook when this boy becomes a teenager. "No, we are not going to eat. We are going to the potty," I tell him. And off we go, with E happily holding my hand on one side, and Daddy's on the other. Once inside, Mommy and Daddy split ways at the restrooms. In retrospect, I am not exactly sure why I didn't send E with his dad to go to the potty. It would have saved me a great deal of embarrassment. And when I say great deal, I mean, what did I call it earlier? Oh yeah, the most embarrassing moment of my life.

We got into the bathroom and I proceeded to do, well, what you do in the bathroom. I handed E my phone to play with so he would be quiet. I could hear people trickling into the bathroom and all of a sudden, E looked at me and quietly said, "Mommy. Poop!" Remember all those phases I mentioned earlier? There's another one, and it's called the broken-record phase. This is the phase in which a child gets something on his mind and decides to repeat it over and over until the parent acknowledges what the child is saying. So I quietly agreed with him, "Yes, Mommy poops. Just like you. Everybody poops."

"Mommy pooping! Mommy, poop in there!" he exclaimed with excitement. "Yay, Mommy! You poop!" Unfortunately, the acknowledgement of this statement did not suffice to stop him this time.

"Yes, E. Mommy's pooping. Now shhh … be quiet. Put a bubble in your mouth," I said, hoping this technique I learned at Vacation Bible School would be effective. The door opened and I heard more people trickling in.

"Mommy pooping! Mommy pooping! MOMMY POOOOOOOOPING!" Nope, not effective. Not effective at all.

I started hearing giggling in the bathroom. Certainly, they weren't laughing at my most precious son. Maybe somebody said something funny out there that I missed because my son was too busy informing me of my present occupation.

He continued, "MOMMY, POOP IN THERE! POOOOOP IN THERE! YAY, MOMMY! YOU POOPING!"

The people in the bathroom were dying with laughter, and I realized my son was so loud that his declaration could probably be heard within a hundred-mile radius. I began to ponder living out the rest of my life in this bathroom stall. I began to calculate the probability of me surviving this experience with any dignity left, and the chances looked rather slim. At that moment, I decided I was officially stuck in this bathroom forever, because I obviously could never come out, for the sake of said dignity. All the while, E continued to chant, "MOMMY POOP! MOMMY POOP! POOOOOP!"

There was certainly about to be a meltdown of epic proportions. And it wasn't going to be the toddler this time. It was my turn. *Do I cry or laugh?* I really wanted to cry. I really did, but instead I started to laugh. And I started laughing hard, like laughing so hard I couldn't breathe, laughing so hard my mascara was running rather badly, laughing so hard I could barely manage to squeak out an "E! BE QUIET!" which just made the whole bathroom erupt in more laughter.

Seriously, I could have just died. Coming to terms with the fact that I couldn't create a permanent residence in the gas station bathroom, I exited the stall, only to find that the twelve-stalled bathroom was not only completely full, but that the door to the bathroom was OPEN. It was open the entire time during this whole scenario. A line of about twenty very athletic-looking college girls, who must have just come from a sporting event, were all laughing as they stood in a line—a line that went all the way out to the middle of the gas station. And this was not a small gas station. *Really? Was this really happening to me?* Curse you, cruel world!

As I was washing my hands, everyone told me, "Ohhh, he's so cute! He's adorable! He's so cute!"

Yeah, so cute. He'd be cuter if this wasn't happening to me! Okay, they were right. He is really cute, like really, really cute, even if he just announced to a gas station full of college girls that Mommy pooped.

I finally exit the rest room, walking past the long line of girls, and doing my best to not look like I am doing the walk of shame.

Hey girls, everybody poops and one day, you just may be the mother of a toddler, too, and get to experience such embarrassment.

Ah yes, the joys of being a mother. After I got past all the girls who were not at all trying to contain their laughter, my husband walked over to me and saw that my mascara was halfway down my face. "What's wrong? What happened?"

"Let's get out of here. Quickly. I'll tell you in the car once we are far, far away from here!"

As I blotted off the mascara tears, I told my husband what happened, and, of course, he couldn't contain himself either. "I'm so glad I could provide you and the rest of that university sports team some entertainment!"

And here I am now documenting my most embarrassing meltdown moment in a book. You're welcome.

Meltdowns are a part of motherhood, and there is no escaping them. Meltdowns are a part of the parenting package. Some of your child's meltdowns are going to make you cry, and some are going to make you laugh. (Please note: that just makes your child melt even more!) Sometimes your child's outburst will give you meltdowns of your own. But those little people are so worth the meltdowns. I can't begin to describe to you the joy it brings me to be a mom. It is the hardest, happiest, most trying, rewarding, sometimes embarrassing, awesome thing I have ever done in my life. I wouldn't trade it for the world!

So just embrace the fact that you may feel hysterical at times. Embrace the fact that meltdowns are a part of motherhood. And embrace the fact that, at some point, your child may announce to the world that you are pooping.

———————

Stephanie Farley is wife to Dr. Smartypants and mom to a little red-headed boy. She's a Christ follower, a do-it-yourselfer, a list lover, and coffeeaholic. She lives by the slogan: I am Mommy! Hear me roar! She writes to encourage women in their journeys as mothers and wives. When she's not tending to her little ginger's every need, you can find her at Crayon Marks and Tiger Stripes, where she blogs about healthy living, maintaining a positive body image, faith, and the ups and downs of parenting.

BONUS #4

Keeping the Peace: Advice from the Trenches of Elementary School
By Rachel Demas

I smiled when my husband said, "Claire seems so tempestuous, lately."

"Why the smile?" he asked.

I tried to figure out how to say what I was thinking without offending him. Often, when I give my perspective or offer advice about his relationship with our toddler, Claire, he hears it like I'm the know-it-all wife carping at a feckless husband.

"Do you really want to know?" I said.

"Yes," he countered.

"You and Claire fight a lot," I say with trepidation. "You guys get into power struggles. She doesn't want to do stuff that you want her to do, so she yells at you. You force her to do it anyway. She yells louder. You yell back."

"Got any advice?" he says. I've gotten him thinking, instead of defending himself. It's time to bend his ear …

"Sure," I say. After all, I was an elementary education teacher before having Claire. I remind him that the advice I have to offer is based on years of professional experience.

I start with the philosophical, "I'm not talking about the run-of-the-mill tantrum or when kids just want what they want. All young children struggle with emotional regulation, impulse control, and expressing their feelings. We need to teach them how to manage those things in life, too. My advice is about helping you with the emotional dynamic of your relationship with Claire. It's about supporting her sense of agency in relation to your authority over her and making sure she feels respected and seen by you."

Then, I outlined what I had learned in the trenches about the emotional dynamic between adult and child—the down and dirty, the nitty-gritty of keeping the peace in the classroom. Now that I've shared this list with my husband, I've formalized it for all the world to see:

HELP! I NEED SOMEBODY!: Capitalize on your child's desire to help you and to be needed. Sometimes, when Claire starts to struggle against me, I remind her that I need her help to get the task done. I remind her that her shoes will not go on her feet without her. On a good day, she will quickly turn from my foe to my ally. We have now become a team working towards a common good. I always make sure I thank her profusely afterwards for her essential contribution to getting the job done.

FAIR WARNING: Outline expectations for your child ahead of time. My husband is particularly bad about this one. For example, he will expect Claire to abandon the puzzle in which she is completely absorbed, in order to eat lunch. In his mind, he's made her food and it's time to eat. She likes to know what's coming. She can struggle with transitions. If you think about it, adults do, too. Kids appreciate a heads-up about what's coming next on the agenda, just like us.

FEELINGS…NOTHING MORE THAN FEELINGS: We tend to forget that kids want the same thing that we want a lot of the time. They want their experience validated and to feel like we understand them. My interactions with Claire tend to be more peaceful, when I acknowledge her feelings and encourage her. "I know it's hard to wait for breakfast to be ready. Sometimes, I don't like waiting either. You're doing a great job waiting." Not only am I trying to show my child that I see her, I am putting

into words what she probably can't yet.

THE CARROT: I want Claire to learn how to pick up her toys, not generally something that she wants to do. When I dangle the park in front of her, she's more apt to acquiesce. I will say, "It's time to go to the park, but we have to pick up our toys before we go." Works like a charm every time. Of course, eventually I want her to pick up her toys on her own. She isn't there yet. The "carrot" strategy is what we would call "scaffolding" in the educational world. It's a support used in a new area of learning. When she's had enough practice, we will take the scaffold away and see how that goes.

THE TIME IS NOW: Instead of saying, "I want you to eat breakfast" or asking, "Do you want to eat breakfast?" I say, "It's time to eat breakfast." Really, this tweak is a minor sleight of hand. I don't know why it works so well. But blaming your request on *time* instead of *you* takes away the personal element, and, hence, the power struggle. It was one of the first things someone told me as a new teacher. If you go into any class in any part of the country, you will probably see teachers employing this one.

TIMING IS EVERYTHING: When we make a request of a kid, we often assume that he needs to do it right away or we will lose face with him somehow. It's not necessarily true. Kids have a different concept of time, so if there's no urgency, let your little one do it on his own time. You can acknowledge what's going on, "I know you don't want to do this right now, but we need to do it soon." Then, set a timer to remind him that it needs to get done.

READY, SET, GO: Similar to the previous one, when there's no time constraint, ask your child to tell you when she is ready. She just wants to feel some control over her destiny, which is reasonable enough. This strategy works particularly well when your child is close to you with nothing better to do. When Claire doesn't want to have her diaper changed, I will take a step back from the diaper pad and say, "You let me know when you are ready." She gets bored, and it usually isn't long before she thinks it's *her* idea to have her clothes or diaper changed.

PRO-CHOICE: I think most people are aware of this one. When a child is offered a choice, the decision becomes his, instead of something being done to him. It's important to remember to keep the choices simple and limited to a small number though. Too much choice can be overwhelming for a child.

CHOOSE OR LOSE: When you are in a hurry, you can start by offering a choice. If this strategy isn't working or is taking too long, you can say, "If you don't make a choice between x and y, I'm going to make a choice for you." Children don't generally like it when you take charge of the situation, but they seem to have an uncanny, intuitive understanding of the fairness and logic of their loss of choice and are more apt to accept it.

DANGER, WILL ROBINSON: Try keeping the "non-negotiables" limited to dangerous activities and things that you absolutely will not tolerate. Then, kids will take you seriously when you make a "no options" demand of them. It's like the boy who cried wolf. If you cry wolf too many times, they won't believe you when you really mean it.

EVERYTHING BUT THE KITCHEN SINK: What worked yesterday might not work today. You have to be flexible, try different things, try many things, switch it up. Something will usually stick.

ALL IS NOTHING: Sometimes nothing works.

HONESTY IS THE BEST POLICY: So you've tried all of these things and nothing is working. You're late for a doctor's appointment and your child needs to get with the program. Be honest, but keep it brief, factual, and calm. "We need to go to the doctor now. I have to take away your Legos. I know you don't like it. I know you're mad." Then, soothe the angry beast as best you can.

HUMAN NATURE: Cut yourself some slack. You won't be perfect. I'm not. After years of teaching, I still lose my shit. I'm tired, hungry, in a hurry, feeling grumpy. If you don't believe me,

refer to my other piece in this book, where I'm going with tired as my excuse for my mega-meltdown. Remember that kids will not lose their respect for you for being human. You can always talk about your conflict afterward. You can always apologize. Remember it's not the battle, it's the war (not crazy about the "war" analogy, but it does work).

Also, a little bird told me that some of these tips work well on husbands, too. Personally, I can only vouch for their effectiveness with children, but feel free to knock yourself out …

Mommy Berserker Always Knows Best

By Melissa Swedoski
Home on Deranged

"9-1-1. What's your emergency?"

I think I'm having a mental breakdown in the grocery store parking lot. I can't get the damn baby bottle to work, and someone just crashed into me with their cart."

"Excuse me?"

"Dammit, woman! Send the National Guard before this becomes a full-scale riot!"

It could have happened like that. It probably should have happened like that. But it didn't. Instead, it happened like this. And one day, it'll seem funny. One day.

After six years of living in sweltering, hot, ridiculously rural southeast Texas, my husband and I finally sold the small, weekly newspaper that we had nurtured and grown.

With a nine-month-old girl, we were ready for a change of scenery and lifestyle. Annie is a laid-back baby. She isn't in much of a hurry to do anything. My husband is a laid-back guy. He's cool with whatever life throws his way.

And then there's me.

At three-plus months pregnant, I am a crazy person, a hormonal nut job, you might say. This pregnancy has sent me into all shades of insanity, but at least I can usually see when I am being absurd. Usually.

As part of our moving process, we begin purging things that we don't really need or want, including our ridiculously large collection of books. My husband locates a used bookstore in the metropolitan area thirty minutes from where we live, so one early fall day we decide to go and sell the books ... three brown paper shopping bags full of books. Yes, the local grocery store in our town still uses brown paper bags. They are far handier than you may remember.

The bookstore is small, so Annie and I sit in the "kids' corner" as she rifles through books. I pretend to be interested, while the list of 19,000 things I need to do continues to grow in my head.

Annie starts to get a little cranky, but who can blame her? She's in a store that smells of old books. This might be sexy to a bibliophile, but it's not so interesting to an infant.

Like any good mother, I just ignore Annie's crankiness. Most bad moods pass if you just distract the kids. "See? There's a really funny pop-up book. Feel free to destroy it."

Time is crawling. My husband informs me that the clerk has to go through each book, give it the once-over, and then decide on a price. Oh, and we don't get money for these books. Just store credit. So, we're not really getting ahead then, *are we?*

Annie has lost interest in destroying old books. She's mad. She's agitated. She's acting like she's hungry. I glance at my watch. Crap. She is hungry. And this baby does not like to miss a meal.

As I prepare to go ask for car keys, a queasy feeling washes over me. *What is it?* I didn't put bottles in the diaper bag. No, I didn't put diapers in the diaper bag. No, it was the snacks that I forgot to bring.

Oh. My. God. I forgot the freaking diaper bag that is now forty minutes away from us, still resting comfortably on our sofa.

Commence meltdown countdown, T-minus twenty minutes.

I have a slight rush of panic. I immediately begin a rationalization process in which I determine that this isn't as bad

as it seems. It's going to be all right. She'll be satisfied by her pacifier for a little longer, at least until we get home. We can get snacks at the gas station.

You know that nervous, twitchy feeling, like something bubbling up in your stomach, waiting to shove itself up your esophagus? Yep, that's there. And getting more acidic by the minute.

"Honey, um … Annie's hungry."

"You need the car keys?"

"The thing is, I forgot the diaper bag."

Suddenly, I have his full concentration, which is rare for a man with a twenty-second attention span.

"What are you going to do?" he asks, in a slightly panicked voice.

I'm a little taken aback by that question, as I reply, "I thought we'd go home. She can make it thirty more minutes. I think." And as the foolish words tumble out of my mouth, as if on cue, Annie produces a primal scream that either means she's reliving the memory of her last meal or she's going through an exorcism. It's 50/50.

His eyes dart furtively, and I know he's concocting a plan. "The thing is, she's not done with the books."

Are you freaking kidding me? Can you not see that I'm on the edge of a panic attack and a trip to the ER may be at hand? But what I really said was, "I see."

My mind is racing a million miles an hour, trying to contemplate the fourteen different ways this tragedy can end: my child starves to death in literally ten minutes; I pull out all my hair—and eat it—because the stress is too much to bear; my husband continues to be utterly perplexed at what is unfolding before his eyes.

The thing is … I'm the mom. I'm not supposed to forget the fundamental basics: food, diapers, clothes. *Think, woman, think! What would Carol Brady do?*

As if on a Hollywood movie cue, I have an epiphany—there's a grocery store less than a mile down the road. Eureka! Crisis averted! Lord, don't let my daughter have a poopsplosion diaper in the next ten minutes.

Annie is still crying, but fortunately, she loves to ride in the car and is temporarily mollified at the joy of being in the car seat. Again.

I drive a little quickly. Okay, maybe ten miles over the speed limit. It's a big city street. People speed all the time. And this is clearly an emergency. My daughter has already gone through two of the ten minutes it will take for her to starve to death.

Whipping into the parking lot and slinging maybe a wee bit of gravel, I'm fortunate enough to find a spot near the front; which is good, since I'm already sweating from the insane dance I'm doing in my head. Best workout ever.

I grab Annie, who appears to be enjoying this strange little adventure, and head into the grocery store, which is easily three times as big as the store in our little town. It's not that I've never been to a full-grown grocery store. It's that I've never been to this one. Where the hell are the signs that tell you what's in each aisle?

I don't even bother to get a buggy because who has time to strap a baby into the seat? This is an emergency. I can tote Annie around for a few more minutes. Even if she has gone through a growth spurt recently and weighs about five pounds more than last week. Growth spurt? Crap, where's the formula?

My eyes are scanning so quickly, I'm getting a headache from the eye strain of the extreme retina game I'm currently playing. Fortunately, as I look past the checkout lines, I spot the sign at the top of the aisle: BABY.

Thank heavens. Just a few more minutes. I get to the aisle only to be met with perhaps the largest possible variety of baby-related products ever known to man. And not only is the variety of the products overwhelming, the sheer volume of brands makes me want to sit on the floor and cry. Must. Not. Panic.

My eyes dart quickly, looking for the familiar blue and white package. But I need the pre-made bottles. I don't have time to mix stuff. What do I look like? I find the little six pack of the bottles. My brilliant idea—which I wasn't aware that I even had until this very second—is to get the little pre-made product, buy a bottle, and *voila!* Problem solved.

But wait. They don't carry the brand of bottles we use. Don't these people realize how delicate and fragile my child is? She can't use just ANY bottle. Clearly, she is acutely sensitive to such matters. Even if she will eat food off the floor.

Time is slipping by, and yet my feet seem to be steadfastly frozen to this spot on aisle four. No need to panic. More. We can just get a cheap bottle and dispose of it when done. How the heck am I supposed to know what nipple size is on this bottle? For the love of baby feeding, she's already on Level Three. What if it isn't the right size nipple? She could die!

Scratching original plan. Cogitating on new plan. Wait, wait, wait. Don't these pre-made bottles allow for regular nipples? If I just pop out the aluminum top, I can insert the nipple right into place, screw the lid back on, and have my baby fed before she wilts in front of me. Yes, I know she's crawling all over the disgusting grocery store floor. It's because she's desperate and searching for food. Can't you tell she's about to pass out from the exertion? Ignore the fact that she won't stop moving.

Now I just have to find nipples that won't let her drown on too much flow, but won't make her work too hard for her meal. There's one! It claims to be Level Three. I inspect it from top to bottom, through the plastic covering. All right, it'll just have to do.

Scoop up baby, head to register, feeling pretty darn confident. This is a great plan. *Why was I worried?* Maneuver paying while simultaneously holding clearly pissed off daughter (You can't crawl on the grocery store floor all day!) and perhaps the smallest wallet I own, and then head for parking lot.

Putting my precious cargo in the driver's seat, I first get out a nipple so I can pop it right in once I push out this aluminum covering on the bottle top. Just like this. Like. This. I'm poking furiously at this stupid round metal piece. Why won't it come out? I can feel my heart start to race. Don't panic.

I push and push. I try another bottle. And another bottle. And another bottle. Isn't the definition of insanity to keep doing the same thing over and over while expecting a different outcome? Then I'm about to lose my mind in the Market Basket parking lot.

Annie has reached her breaking point. She's hungrier than she is curious about the inner workings of our car. She's moving into the hysterical wail that only babies and cats with puncture wounds can create. She's wiggling, crying, and the look on her face says, "You betrayed me, Mommy."

How the hell is a person supposed to get the metal ring out so you can slip in the nipple? I'm so mad at this bottle, I'm prepared to hurl it all the way across the parking lot. Instead, I opt for shaking the crap out of it. I. Am. About. To. Lose. My. Shit. What the hell is wrong with you, bottle?

I move Annie to the passenger seat. I don't have time for car seats, dammit, this is an emergency of epic proportions. She's still crying, but she's momentarily entertained by the change of scenery. I get into the driver seat, but before I close the door, I see it … the special Swiss Army Knife keychain I bought my husband for Christmas, complete with teeny-tiny knives and tools, as well as a flash drive for transporting international secret codes about spies.

I'll just cut out the metal covering and we're back in business. Find teeny-tiny knife that looks sharp and commence cutting. Now. Okay, now. Are you kidding me? I stab at it. I punch at it. It will not budge. I turn it over and attack it from behind. I finally get the knife to penetrate the metal, leaving what essentially looks like an air hole for mice I'm keeping in a jar. I try to continue the cut from the breathing hole, but instead, the knife seems to be

getting duller by the nanosecond.

Oh. Holy. Crap. My mind is spinning, I'm sweating profusely, my daughter is chewing on what I hope to heavens is a leftover piece of candy, and I can feel a mental snap coming on in 5 … 4 … 3 … *bam*! What the hell? I look up to realize someone has just nailed our car with a shopping cart. And not in an accidental, oh-so-sorry kind of way. More like a you-were-annoying-me-so-I-hit-you kind of way.

And then it happens. I morph into Mommy Berserker mode. Much like her video game counterpart, Mommy Berserker can spin around really fast, make glass-shattering noises, and shoot balls of fire out of her hands. Okay, I can't do that last part, but I've been told that I have a pretty powerful death stare when I'm pissed off.

The guy tries to just shrug, smile sheepishly, and walk off. Oh, hell no, son, that ain't the way Mommy Berserker plays. Get back in your corner of the ring, cause I'm about to go Rocky on your ass.

Well, that's what I would say, if I was a clever woman in a movie. Instead I say—in a high pitched, quivery voice, no less—something more along the lines of, "You *&#%*#! idiot! How hard is it to navigate a $%^*^% shopping cart? This isn't NASCAR, you moron! You're lucky I don't call the *^$#^* police on your ass!"

He is either laughing or crying as he walks away. It's hard to say, because Mommy Berserker doesn't have a good frame of reference. I just want someone to let loose my frustrations on, free from the bonds of logic or reason. Or deodorant. Oh my lord, I am sweating. My head is spinning so fast, I can hear the blood rushing in my ears. I glance at my daughter, who mostly just looks very confused by this public display.

As I start to calm down, she resumes crying. And Mommy Berserker gets back up off her flaming throne of rest. "What in the hell were these *&^$#^ formula makers thinking? This isn't easy to use at all! Where are the people I can punish?" Some more curse words fly, as my mind races around to all the angry letters, emails, phone calls, and press releases I could send about this debacle of the formula industry. Frauds.

Because the car door is open, I'm pretty sure some other people got to see this public display. Again, Mommy Berserker doesn't really notice what's going on around her. She's got tunnel vision, which only includes her child—who is about to starve because of these stupid formula companies!

It's time for Plan B. My husband is stronger than I am, and he'll be able to push out this metal demon keeping my child from food. But wait. I have a brilliant idea. She can drink from a cup, sort of. I'll just let her drink formula straight from this pre-made bottle, which is a heck of a lot different than drinking water—especially when you don't have a diaper bag with burp cloths and bibs. And you don't have any towels or napkins in the car. All you have is tissues, which essentially disintegrate when they are touched by the formula. It wouldn't be the first time she's had to wear her meal for a while.

Annie drinks just enough to satiate her until we can get back to the bookstore, my port in the storm. She is lying in the front seat, as I have my right hand splayed across her belly. I'm attempting to make right and left turns with one hand, while keeping her from rolling onto the floorboard. I miss the turn for the bookstore and have to make a one-handed U-turn. I am losing my mind, but Mommy Berserker is well in control. She can run red lights, flip off other drivers, and still hold a baby down with one hand.

We reach the bookstore, as I run up, fling open the door, and, without any thought of civility, loudly screech, "Thomas! I need your help! NOW!" I'm sure he is thrilled with that, as the look on his face indicates he is (not), but when he sees Mommy Berserker has come out to play, he decides to keep his thoughts to himself.

He follows me to the car as I try to explain the evil that is the metal cap on the pre-made formula bottle and that all

I want to do is feed our starving daughter and this demon possessed product won't let me. He looks at it, examines it, looks at me, looks at it again, and in his calmest, I'm-talking-to-a-crazy-person voice says, "Honey, it doesn't come out. You're not supposed to be able to remove it and put a nipple in. You have to pour it into something else."

Ever watched a balloon plummet to earth after you pop it with a pin? I'm guessing that's what I looked like, slumping back in the driver's seat. I look over at our daughter, who has been entertaining herself by gnawing on her dad's set of keys, which included a blue canvas keychain. Her face is covered in blue. Along with her tongue. I want to laugh, but Mommy Berserker is holding tight to the reins.

"Why the hell not? Why didn't I notice that? Are you sure you can't make it work? You can fix everything! She can't drink from a cup well enough yet for this to work!"

Mommy Berserker leans out to shake him. "Don't you understand how &^$#^ important this is? My "Awesome Mommy" badge is in danger of being revoked!"

He suggests that Annie and I get out of the car and sit on the store steps, and as I sit, he hands her to me, offering the bottle of formula right after. "I'll keep trying," he says. "That's a lot of holes you've made."

Mommy Berserker does not need a smartass right now. She's still ready to tear someone a new one. She's fired off fifteen furious complaint letters in her head already. They are so going to be sorry for what they did.

I sit on the steps, gently trying to get my daughter to drink from the bottle, with its oversize opening. She does pretty well … because she's a genius, of course. Mommy Berserker's tunnel vision is still set to "on," and Annie is the only other thing I can see in the universe at this moment. At some point, my husband hands me a bottle with a nipple on it. I don't know how he did it. And he says gently, "It doesn't fit perfectly, so you'll still need to hold it for her."

And finally, Mommy Berserker withdraws her claws back into her hands, lets the horns on her head retract, allows the fire in her eyes to extinguish, and then turns off the tunnel vision, so I can see what's happening. Or, more accurately, what just happened. Did I seriously just make a scene in the Market Basket parking lot? Um … yeah.

As I slowly spiral back to earth, it occurs to me *why didn't I just buy a couple of jars of baby food and a spoon, since she can already eat solids?* Because Mommy Berserker is always right. And the National Guard was busy.

After a career as a newspaper reporter and editor, Melissa Swedoski thought she was well-informed on the chaos of everyday life. Then she married a man thirteen years her junior and became a SAHM to two toddler girls. Now, she's mumbling through the mayhem of marriage and motherhood in a small Texas town, turning her investigative eye on the mishaps and misadventures of parenting, and the marathon that is marriage, always with the emphasis on humor and love. You can find her living her big little life at Home on Deranged.

I'm Not Pregnant, I'm Fat

By Melissa Galileo
Completely Eclipsed

As I sat in the passenger seat of our sensible, mid-sized SUV, I looked down at my toes and frowned. They were painted lovingly by my four-year-old daughter Isabella in a charming pattern of red and neon orange. She's a sweet girl, but has the fashion sense of a gypsy gone rogue. As we approached the nail salon, I was practically giddy with excitement, not only because the state of my toes would shortly be vastly improved, but also because right after getting that much-needed pedicure, my husband and I were going away for two whole days.

We hadn't had a full night's rest since my second daughter, Arya, was born three months earlier. We were tired and pushed to the brink of exhaustion and frustration by the needs of a newborn and by Isabella's incessant talking. *Seriously, do four-year-olds come with a mute button?* I was so beyond ready to have two blissful days to myself, to not have a wee nursling constantly hanging off my boob or diapers to change or crusts to cut off of sandwiches that never get eaten anyway. I was ready. But if I was going to be seen out in public with other adults, I'd need to first take care of the state of my toes.

My husband, Andy, pulled into the nail salon and told me that he'd pick me up after he ran a few errands. I told him to take his time because just the idea of sitting down and reading a book that didn't have pictures in it was enough to blow my mind. In the nail salon I browsed a rainbow of shades before settling on one that was neither red, nor neon orange, sat down in the plush leather chair, opened up my book, and let go.

"You look really beautiful," the lady who was hacking away at the calluses on my heels said to me in very broken English.

I beamed. I mean I was three months postpartum, and things were not exactly bouncing back as quickly as they had with my first. I was still largely wearing yoga pants, leggings, and maternity jeans. I was feeling very self-conscious about my body and how soft it was. I'd been especially down on myself because of my inability to stick with a diet longer than an afternoon, and the majority of my attempts at running ended with me shoving a Pop-Tart down my throat twenty minutes later. So when this woman offered up a compliment to me so freely, it really made me swell with happiness.

"Thank you so much! I really appreciate that," I said with a smile.

"No, I mean it, you look so good."

"Thank you!" I replied, mentally calculating if there was enough money in my bank account to tip this woman a million dollars. Then I remembered that I'm a teacher and I have no money.

"When is your due date?"

I deflated.

This woman, who I was practically ready to throw my life savings at, thought I was pregnant. And not just pregnant, but far enough along that she felt comfortable asking when I was due. She thought I was at least five months pregnant. I could feel the tears start to sting my eyes like red-hot pokers of shame. I had a lump in my throat the size of a golf ball. *Don't lose it right now, Melissa, pull yourself together,* I told myself.

I took a deep breath, swallowed my tears and my pride, and curtly said, "I'm not pregnant." This woman was getting lint for a tip.

I looked around to see how many witnesses there were to this epic humiliation. There was a girl sitting next to me who couldn't have been a day over seventeen and who probably weighed about ninety pounds soaking wet. She had her face deeply buried in her magazine, and I silently thanked her for having the good grace to pretend that she hadn't just heard what she clearly did. And they say the youth of America is in peril.

The rest of my pedicure was endured in a sort of stunned silence and as soon as she was done, I made a mad dash to the bathroom so I could look at myself in the mirror and decide for myself if I looked pregnant.

Well, the bathroom was the size of a broom closet and the mirror the size of a postage stamp. Not to be deterred, I climbed up on the toilet seat, one foot balanced on the lid and the other braced against the sink. For a moment I slightly considered the possibility that I would rip the sink from the wall. I'm sure that would have made everyone happy. "The fat/pregnant lady just ripped out a plumbing fixture!" But I needed to see my stomach. I needed to see if what she saw was true. I was a woman crazed, and I needed to look in that mirror and see what she saw.

I hoisted up my nursing tank and slightly stretched out T-shirt and I looked at my body; there in that tiny bathroom shrouded in shame and embarrassment, I looked. I wilted at what I saw. My stomach was soft, like bread dough, angry red stretch marks raced across my middle, my belly button looked like a stretched out butthole, and a jagged linea nigra ran from pubic bone to belly button. My hips muffin-topped over the waistband of my pants. I couldn't see my thighs in the tiny mirror, but I knew they hadn't fared much better.

I tried to give myself a pep talk. I really did try. I tried to look at my body and tell myself that I just had a baby three short months ago, that my body had carried a life inside of it for over forty weeks, that it had stretched as my baby grew, and that my body was currently making milk to nourish that sweet life. I tried to tell myself that my hips had widened during a labor that was so fast, so furious that I practically crawled into the hospital. I tried to summon up pictures that I've seen of women on Pinterest likening their stretch marks to "tiger stripes." I don't care what fancy words you use to name them, they still aren't pretty, and even though I intellectually understood all that I was trying to convince myself of, I was completely being ruled by my emotions. Also, part of me knew that it wasn't all from the baby, that I had let my eating and lack of exercise grow from a grace period into a way of life. I understood that I couldn't just blame the baby—that I had to take some ownership and responsibility over my body.

With my head hung, I quickly left the bathroom, paid, and left.

As soon as I got in the car, my husband could tell something was off.

"What happened?" he asked. "Did they mess up your toes or something?"

"No, no I'm fine," I lied. I really did not want to have to rehash the entire ordeal. My husband loves me more than anything, no matter what size I am, but I'm also not stupid and I know he isn't blind. Maybe he also thought I looked pregnant and was just too polite to say something.

His brows furrowed in that way where he's not sure if he should push me or leave me be. "We can go to Chipotle for lunch if you'd like," he offered.

I said *yes* without hesitation, and then I immediately kicked myself. I tend to eat my feelings, and I was definitely having a lot of feelings. I also figured that I could swing by the department store and pick up some heavy duty SPANX, which they make in industrial strength for situations just like this.

We rode in silence to the mall, but once I got a little food in me I started feeling less embarrassed and angrier. It's like each delicious bite of my burrito was turning all of those negative thoughts into rage. I mean honestly, what woman makes a pregnancy comment to another woman like that? That's like Girl

101. Unless a woman explicitly tells you that she's pregnant or you physically see the baby coming out of her, you keep your mouth shut. Everybody knows that. The more I thought about it, the angrier I got. Who was this woman to make me feel bad about myself? Why does society expect women to bounce back into fighting shape after having a baby? Because the latest celebrity did? Maybe I don't go for regular runs, because I'd rather take a nap after pacing the floors with a crying baby all night. Maybe I pick up fast food more than I should, because I'd rather give my oldest daughter a little one-on-one attention than cooking in the kitchen.

I had just reached my mental breaking point, and I could feel my blood begin to boil. I was on the brink of a full-fledged mommy meltdown.

"I need to go back to the nail salon. I left my credit card there," I said.

My husband just kind of rolled his eyes at my forgetfulness and took me back. I walked into that store full of piss and vinegar, and I zeroed in on the woman who had helped me earlier.

"Um, hi," I started once I realized that I was standing in the middle of a semi-crowded nail salon and everyone was staring at me. "I was in here earlier and you asked me when my baby was due, but I'm not pregnant. That is an incredibly rude and ignorant question to ask of a woman. As a woman yourself, you should know better. For your information I just had a baby three months ago, and I haven't had the time or energy to lose all the weight yet. I shouldn't have to feel bad about myself all day because you asked a ridiculously insensitive question."

In one epic breath I said all of that, everything I had been thinking, and for the briefest of moments I felt vindicated. Then I realized how absolutely insane I must have looked and how, at that moment, everyone in the salon was probably staring at my flabby, deflated stomach and asking themselves, "Does she look pregnant or not?" And I was instantly mortified. I could feel my face burning scarlet and my ears had gone completely fuzzy. I turned on my heel and hauled ass out of that nail salon as fast as I could without even hearing her response. I like to think that the women in the salon started a slow clap for me and my bravery, but it was more likely that they just updated their Facebook statuses about some verifiable nutcase who had interrupted their manicures.

I now drive an extra ten minutes and pay an extra two bucks to get my nails done.

Melissa Galileo is a New York City elementary school teacher. She has taught in the inner city for the past nine years and is committed to helping her students become great readers and writers. Melissa lives in New Jersey with her husband and two young daughters. She is also the wine-drenched mind behind Completely Eclipsed, where she writes about her warts-and-all experiences with motherhood and life in general. She does not craft, bake, or sew, but she has a healthy addiction to Pinterest and coffee.

Let's Pretend This Never Happened

By Jennifer Barbour
Another Jennifer

*I*t was one of those perfect weather days. Not too hot, not too cold. The sun lightly warmed your skin. A delicate breeze made you want to breathe in the fresh and undeniably comfortable air and let it envelope the insides of your body.

If you were alive, you wanted to be outside. It was a struggle to bring the dogs inside when I left the house to pick up my sons after what seemed like a long day in my home office.

G got off the elementary school bus as usual. He gave me the full report of what he did that day in second grade on the short walk back to the house. "Nothing too exciting."

We hopped in the car and headed to daycare to pick up his younger brother.

This was the typical schedule during the school year. In the time between the drop-off in the morning and the pickup in the afternoon, I crammed as much as I could in for work—meetings, writing, coaching sessions—to minimize the time I had to work at night.

But I almost always end up working at night; such is the life of an entrepreneur. It's the moments between school/daycare pickup and bedtime that are the most precious and relaxing to me. The time with my family helps me keep things in perspective. On a good day at least.

I could sense trouble from the moment I arrived at daycare. I caught a glimpse of the top of my three-year-old son's head as I stepped out of the car. As I walked to the gate, I could tell he was aware of my presence and not happy about it. He continued to play in the sandbox, completely ignoring me and his little friends who were now loudly yelling, "Biz, your mom's here!"

He wasn't ready to leave and I was fine with that. I had been doing the daycare thing with my kids for seven years at that point, so I knew the drill. I just needed to give him a few moments to finish up his play, and then I could start coaxing him, gently, to leave.

It was a nice day. I wouldn't want to leave either.

I know about these transitions at the beginning and end of daycare. I was a pro at the "dump and run" when my boys were younger. Though it tore me to pieces the first few times I had to do it, I could kiss my kids good-bye as they screamed for me and tried desperately to grasp at me as I walked out the door. I would remain stone-faced and didn't even cry until I drove down the street.

The women at my daycare would call me an hour later to tell me that my boys stopped crying the moment I left the building. Part of me was proud to have such happy, well-adjusted kids who could handle such tough transitions at a young age. The other part of me wondered why the heck they didn't care that their mom just left them for the day.

Today, I am an occasional counselor to some of the newbie moms and dads who struggle with the newness of leaving their kids at daycare. It's always harder on you, I tell them. I tell them how to do the dump and run and assure them that they aren't scarring their kids for life. We're usually hiding from our kids during these conversations, hoping they don't see us lingering in the parking lot.

I've read, in all the parenting magazines and websites, all the tips and tricks to helping kids transition from one moment to the next. I knew the strategies to use when we were leaving a

playground, getting ready for dinner, or picking up at daycare. I was a well-informed mother. Except every now and then, those strategies didn't work with my younger son.

On that warm spring day, my presence was the worst thing that had happened to him in recent history. He moved from the sandbox to the playground behind the daycare without any acknowledgment of my presence. With his back to me, he stood with a look of utter disgust on his face. It was similar to the look I made when I was enjoying an expensive dinner and the perfect glass of wine and received a text from the babysitter that asked what to do about our oldest dog being sprayed by a skunk.

"Hi, Biz!" I called over to him, with as much enthusiasm as I could muster.

He ignored me and stomped away.

"Why don't you finish up playing and we'll leave in a few minutes," I said to him and started to chit-chat with one of the daycare workers.

My presence and the intention of leaving were on record. I was good for a few minutes.

At that moment, however, I lost G. Being a former member of the daycare, he was kind of a legend there. He was now the big kid that all the little girls wanted to chase once he walked through the gate. He zoomed by me occasionally, trailed by his giggling fan club.

"G, you need to help me get Biz out of here, remember?" We've had the conversation about leaving when I say we're going to leave so Biz will follow numerous times.

G didn't hear any of my gentle requests to stop running and concentrate on leaving the premises.

Biz had moved from the backyard to the driveway and was now riding with reckless abandon on a bike. Shooting an occasional dirty look my way as he rode by, he showed no signs of stopping and complying with my requests to leave.

Suddenly the sun started to feel warmer on my skin and I began to sweat. My gentle reminders of going home started to become more urgent, and I moved on to new departure strategies.

"One more run and ride around and then we're leaving!"

"We'll play in the sandbox when we get home and we can make a big castle!"

"If you don't go home with me, you won't get to play with your new car!"

"The dogs need to go outside!"

"If you don't listen, you'll be in a timeout when we get home!"

"Mommy needs to get home to start dinner!"

The last one was in pure desperation since my husband is the one that cooks dinner. It was a good test to see if the boys were listening though. They were not.

Seeing my struggles, the daycare workers attempted to move my kids along. "Listen to your mother, boys. We'll see you tomorrow!"

At this point, other mothers were arriving to scoop up their beaming children after a long day at work. Those children anxiously awaited their parent's arrival to the gate, hardly containing their excitement while wildly squealing things like, "Mommy's here!"

Would it kill my kids to be excited to see me? I thought. The perfect day was quickly becoming a perfect disaster.

"OK, G and Biz, we're done," I boldly stated. "I'm leaving with or without you." I gave the other parents a sly smile as I walked towards the gate. I knew what I was doing.

Except that my kids didn't budge. I don't think G heard me at all, and I'm pretty sure Biz waved good-bye to me. The daycare workers and other parents respectfully kept out of the debacle and left me on my own to handle the situation.

Though I picked up earlier than many of the other parents, the daycare was beginning to thin out. I was convinced I would never leave that property with my kids.

It was time for a new strategy.

"I guess you're sleeping here tonight," I said with a nervous smile as I slunk out through the gate and started to walk to the

car. I looked behind me and saw that G had started to catch on. Biz blissfully pedaled away on his bike as one of the daycare workers told him he needed to listen to his mother.

Despite everyone's best efforts, there was still no movement towards the gate. I guess all that dumping and running made them a bit too comfortable with me leaving them.

I was finally able to get them into the car with one last, stern warning. Biz, though reluctant, skipped along to the car as if nothing had happened. G, on the other hand, could sense my annoyance. He knows when Mom's about to go off the deep end.

I couldn't have been at that daycare for more than fifteen to twenty minutes, but it felt like a lifetime. I tried every trick in the book and neither one of my boys cooperated. All I wanted to do was leave. After a busy day of work, I just wanted to unwind and hang out with my kids. Apparently that was too much to ask for. Or so it seemed. In my stressed-out state, I wasn't exactly thinking clearly. And I certainly didn't stop to think about how nice it was to have a daycare where my kids felt so comfortable.

What happened next is a bit of a blur. I remember making sure my kids were safely buckled into the car, taking a deep breath, and waving good-bye to the remaining people outside the daycare. I put on the best smile I could muster as I drove away.

I made it to the end of the road and then I unleashed on my kids. I mean, really unleashed. I started yelling loudly about how disrespectful it was to not listen to me. How I asked them about a million times to leave and they completely ignored me. How it made me sad that they weren't happy to see me. How I work the schedule I do so that I can spend more time with them and they didn't even care. I'm pretty sure I dropped an F-bomb or two in my mini-tirade. I topped it all off with a good cry.

That perfect day produced the perfect storm. Yelling. Swearing. Crying. It was the trifecta of bad mothering. Of course, let's not forget about the good old-fashioned guilt trip I laid on them.

Luckily, the ride from daycare to home is short. It takes about three and a half minutes, depending on how long you have to sit at the traffic light. My mom-guilt started seeping in midway through my meltdown, spurring the shower of tears. By the time I parked the car in the garage, my kids sat stunned and upset. If I remember correctly—again, this was all a blur to me—they were crying along with me.

G stepped up and apologized for their behavior. "We love you, Mommy," he told me. Those words made me sob even more.

"I'm sorry for yelling, but Mommy's upset right now," I told them. "I don't want to talk to anyone right now. We're all going in a timeout."

The boys went to their rooms and I let the dogs outside. I calmed myself down and wondered how I would get myself out of the mess I had created. Surely, my children would look back on this day and use it as an example of how not to parent. Surely, they would be afraid of me now and question my love for them.

After a while, I went upstairs to have an honest talk about what happened. I told them why I was upset and noted that I *might* have overreacted just a tad. We talked about expectations for the next pickup. We made a deal that when I said we were going to leave, they would leave. I was feeling pretty good. Like I turned a mommy meltdown into a lesson in life.

After a few hugs, they started to get antsy. I didn't think our conversation was over, but Biz couldn't take it anymore.

"Mommy, can we go downstairs and watch a show now?"

"Sure. You can both go down …"

Before I could answer the question, they sprung up and bolted down the stairs like nothing had happened.

No scarring. No resentment. No anger towards Mom at all. My meltdown was a reaction to all my perceived stresses in life. It was all in my head. The perfect storm of emotions on an otherwise perfect day.

On second thought, forget about that lesson in life. Let's pretend this never happened.

Deal?

Jennifer Barbour is a professional writer and new media marketing consultant. Based in Brunswick, Maine, she's the proud mom of two boys and three dogs. Jennifer is the author of the Another Jennifer blog, curator of All Things Left-Handed, and creator of the Simple Giving Lab. She writes for Mom Bloggers for Social Good and is the Philanthropy Editor at pplkind. Her passions are writing, philanthropy, her awesome family, and bacon, though not necessarily in that order.

The Backpack that Broke the Mama's Back

By Angela Keck
Writer Mom's Blog

As meltdowns go, I suppose this one started out much like any other, in that it started out like any other day and built into ... well, a meltdown!

The day started with the typical morning insanity of getting both kids ready for school and then dropped off at different schools, on opposite sides of town, twenty minutes apart from each other.

That's where the word "typical" went out the window on this particular day.

After dropping the kids off at school my next stop was Walmart, because no one in my house can be bothered to tell me that we are completely and totally out of toilet paper until we're down to our last square. Literally. So I rush into the store to grab my necessities and decide to pamper myself by also grabbing a bottle of my favorite wine. I'm already excited and anticipating that hour after both kids go to bed when the house is quiet and I can sit back, pour myself a glass of wine, zone out in front of some mindless TV, and relax.

I cursed myself, right there. *Do you see it?*

As I'm rushing out of the store, back to my car, so that I can be home in time for my daily morning staff meeting/conference call at 9:15 a.m., I realize that my keys are not in my purse. They are not in my pocket. They are … in the car!

The only way this moment could have been worse is if there had been a crack of thunder and lightning at the exact moment I realized my keys were locked in the car. Sadly, I don't live on a Hollywood movie set, so I didn't have any special effects. I also didn't have any rain, for which I did say a grateful *thank you*!

So there I stood in the middle of the Walmart parking lot, with my gigantic package of toilet paper and my $5 bottle of wine, unable to get into my car. I call the hubby who informs me that there's no way he can get anywhere near where I am until sometime after 1:00 p.m. He *thinks* his spare key to my car is at home, but he's not sure.

I use my "phone a friend' option and beg a girlfriend to come pick me up, run me to my house, and let me see if I can get inside to look for the spare key. My girlfriend, God bless her, shows up with her two kids (both under five) in her van, still in their pajamas. She runs me home, where I manage to jimmy open a window and climb inside—because it's not just my car keys that are in the car!

Now, if my husband's spare key had been inside the house, this story probably wouldn't result in a meltdown, but would rather be a funny story I would tell you while I shared that bottle of wine I so proudly treated myself to. But, of course, you already know that isn't how this story is going to end. The key is not at home, and I end up begging for a ride back to Walmart from my friend who kindly sits and waits with me while I call a locksmith and pay $50 to get into my own car. Luckily the wait time for the locksmith and the conference call were identical, so my friend and her kids now have had the pleasure of not only waiting with me in the parking lot, but listening in as I attend a work meeting. My friend is clearly the one who deserves the wine in this story!

Fast forward through what is your typical, frenzied pace of a work-from-home day to 3:00 p.m. when I get to repeat my morning run and pick both kids up from their opposite-end-of-town schools within twenty minutes of each other. We rush through dinner, do homework, and get my daughter to her dance class on time. All the while I'm thinking, *I can't believe I had to spend $50 to get into my own car, and I can't wait until I get to pop open that bottle of $5 wine and RELAX on the couch!* I'm practically drooling for that one glass at this point, as much as I am the peace and quiet!

Fast forward to around 9:00 p.m. when we're finally back home after an evening spent watching my daughter dance and keeping my ten-year-old son entertained. By entertained I mean he's managed to drain the battery on my phone completely at least once and then had to sit next to an outlet to keep the phone alive long enough to continue playing Chasing Yello or MineCraft or whatever it was that kept him out of my hair for a few minutes.

I'm beyond exhausted, and ready to collapse into a heap on the couch with that bottle of wine and the remote control!

I hurry inside, ordering the boy child to take a shower because he smells like a ten year old boy. I remind the girl child that she needs to get her PE uniform out of the dryer so she can dress out for PE tomorrow and to gather up her homework off the kitchen table before she heads into her room. I'm in the kitchen hurriedly cleaning up the dinner dishes and fantasizing about that glass of wine.

The kids are grumbling because they share a bathroom, which my teenage daughter is sure is punishment for some kind of horrible sin in a past life. He touched her towel—no, he didn't. He takes too long in the bathroom—he can't help it! He's a slob—she gets hair everywhere! It goes on and on until I threaten both of them that if I hear one more word ... ugh! The look of pain on their faces at not being able to have the last word is almost worth it. Almost.

Finally, dinner is cleaned up. The dishwasher is running. The dog has been let out and back inside. The boy child has showered and is ready for bed. I've poured a glass of wine and I head to the couch.

This is when the real meltdown starts because I discover there is literally not one square inch of available space on the couch for me to sit down. Despite being reminded to gather up their things for school the next morning, despite the fact that we have a HUGE sectional sofa, despite the fact that I've been drooling over this five minutes of relaxation all day long, there is nowhere for me to sit down!

The boy child's backpack is on one end of the couch, with its contents spread out over one half. He is parked right at the end, watching SpongeBob SquarePants as if he doesn't know it's time for bed.

The girl child's backpack and contents are all over the ottoman, and she has her behind parked in my usual spot with her feet propped up right on top of all the stuff she has strewn across the seat.

I literally cannot believe my eyes!

As if this isn't bad enough, I'm ready to collapse into an exhausted heap on the couch after a totally craptastic day, and my kids are sitting there with their feet propped up ignoring all the things I asked them to do before they went to bed; not to mention ignoring the fact that they need to go to bed at all.

I manage to calmly say, "Can you pick up your stuff and get ready for bed?" I am really, truly proud of myself for maintaining my sense of calm at this point. I mean, I didn't yell, I didn't raise my voice, and I didn't spill my wine. Instead I calmly asked them to consider their actions and make better choices.

I am clearly awesome!

And yet, nobody moved.

I wondered if perhaps I had forgotten to actually speak out loud. Maybe I had just *thought* about asking them to pick up their stuff? Yeah, that must be it, because why else would they act as if no one had spoken?

So I repeat my question, and my daughter looks at me and says, "Where do you want me to put it?"

Cue the meltdown.

I set my glass of untouched wine down on the table and proceed to clear myself a spot to sit ... by throwing everything that was on the couch across the room.

It was one of those almost out-of-body experiences where I knew I was acting like a complete and total lunatic, but I couldn't stop myself. The genie was out of the bottle, folks!

The backpack went flying against the living room wall, the shoes—yes, there were shoes on my couch—went right behind them! Pencils and worksheets, empty snack containers, and assorted trash—it all went across the room!

The only point where sanity briefly returned was when something that I tossed across the room knocked a knickknack off the shelf, and I realized I was just making more work for myself because I was just going to have to clean it all up, too!

The kids, clearly shell-shocked, grabbed what they could and ran for their lives mumbling, "Okay, okay we'll pick up, geez," as they took their stuff into their rooms.

The real problem here was that it was April, almost the end of the school year, and every day, all year long, I had said, "Please don't leave your backpack on the couch. The couch is for sitting and your backpack does not need a chair. Take it to your room." Every. Single. Day.

And yet, here was my couch completely covered with backpacks and their contents!

After I had thrown nearly everything I could across the room and yelled about how ungrateful my children were and I finally had a spot to sit down on, I did just that. I sat down, I propped my feet up on the ottoman, I grabbed the glass of wine I'd been thinking about since 8:30 a.m. that morning, and I turned the channel from SpongeBob to something I wanted to watch.

It felt good. It also felt quite ridiculous, but I went with the good feeling.

I told my kids, who had suddenly returned, that they had better go to their bedrooms and not come out until morning, and they mumbled, "Okay, okay," and off they went.

I enjoyed my glass of wine and went to bed, still silently fuming to myself. Hubby was already sleeping soundly and had no idea that I had melted all over the living room floor. I laid there next to him silently thinking how dare he sleep while I was dealing with … well, everything! Why hadn't he cleaned up the dinner dishes before he went to bed? All I had really wanted was five minutes to myself. *Was that asking too much?*

The meltdown continues!

So the next morning when I called him, as I did every morning, I proceeded to fill him in on my meltdown. He listened quietly as I ranted and raved about how all I wanted was to sit down for five minutes and the kids had their stuff everywhere! I told him how I threw things all over the room and the kids thought I was crazy, but they had put their stuff away finally! I told him how it was ridiculous that it took me completely freaking out and losing my cool for anyone else in the house to pitch in and help out!

After I finished telling my story, Hubby calmly said, "And how do you feel now? Better?"

Clearly he was not listening at all!

Angela Keck is thrilled to have turned her passion for online communities and social media into an amazing career. Blogging is a natural extension of her two loves, social media and writing. You can find her blogging about social media, parenting, photography, recipes, and whatever else sparks her fancy at Writer Mom's Blog. Angela owes her return to her first love of writing to the birth of her daughter, who is now fourteen years old. When her daughter was an infant, Angela realized she could not teach her children to chase their dreams if she had given up on her own! So she dusted off her muse and wrote, and wrote, and wrote! When her son was born, ten years ago, she switched from working outside the home to working from home managing online communities. Now she proudly writes between chauffeuring her two children to their activities so they can also chase their dreams. Angela and the love of her life are happily raising their two children, a German shepherd, and one very fat cat in Southern Illinois.

Where's the Cheese?

By Christine Carter
The Mom Cafe

Moms are the QUEENS of multi-tasking, *aren't we?* We are everywhere: at the stores, the schools, the parks, at work, and at home. We juggle all the various balls that get pitched to us in the game we call "motherhood." And this League ain't easy. Moms don't go through any real training for it, although there are some serious hazing rituals of pregnancy many poor souls have to endure. When motherhood hits, the balls start flying high and fast. How we are able to handle it all is truly a mystery. To some it comes so naturally. To others, it's a bit distressing to be so distracted. I tend to be the distressed and distracted mom more often than less.

I can only juggle a few things at a time, or I start to get over-stimulated and overwhelmed. I see other moms with an amazing ability to master this art as they go at top speed with full-throttle focus on several tasks at a time … *incredible*. I am in awe of how one of my friends can literally pick kids up at soccer, run to the grocery store, and get kids home to bed—all the while having a two-hour, meaningful conversation with me on the phone. I didn't even KNOW my friend was doing all of that during the phone call until I said, "I better let you go so you can get back to the kids." She replied, "Oh I am home now from doing everything and the kids are fine." Wow.

When *I* am on the phone, I wave my hand frantically, silently mouthing a screaming tirade for my kids to *Get. Away. Now.* And then after that, I have to ask the caller to repeat everything she said during that time! Geez. Just too much.

Other plays in the motherhood playbook are a bit more tolerable to me. Not that they are easy, but I feel quite competent, which if you are a mom, is a very rare thing. The after-school frenzy is always a crazy mess. I can muster the ability to handle the balls flyin' at top speed most days.

But then I have a day like this ...

After idling my car at the school pick-up line for three hours (slight exaggeration only), my kids come flying into the house, opening backpacks, and hurling papers and rancid lunchboxes onto the kitchen counter. My daughter is starving and begging for a grilled cheese sandwich. While catching a flying packet, I feel my phone buzz with a text from a dear friend who is in a crisis. I start to counsel (text therapy rocks!) as my daughter painfully reminds me that she will literally DIE if she doesn't get a grilled cheese in her stomach, STAT. (Poor, poor child!) I frantically pull out the makings of a grilled cheese, while I tell her to go pick some grass and eat it so she can relate to the rest of the starving children in the world. (Sarcasm is a healthy alternative to rage.)

The kids are running through the house and back outside, in and out ... screaming ... in and out, fighting over something ridiculous. I continue to text with my friend as my heart breaks for her. On the skillet ... flip ... pat ... get plates, drinks, text again ... text again ... flip ... done! *STOP YELLING! COME GET YOUR GRILLED CHEESE!* As my daughter comes in and grabs her sandwich, I start to clean up the kitchen and sort the mounds of papers remaining on the counter as I pray for my friend. *AND CLOSE THE DOOR!* I call as my kids run outside to play and fight as only siblings do.

Five minutes later, my daughter comes back in with a half-eaten sandwich.

"Mommy! Why isn't there any cheese in my grilled cheese?"

Oops.

Yep. I made a grilled cheese sandwich with no cheese. Perhaps the worst part of this story is that I told her she could still eat it like toast. And after she whined about that, I told her it was better than eating grass.

Yes, I did.

Chris Carter is a SAHM of two pretty amazing grade-school kids. She has been writing at The Mom Cafe for almost three years, where she hopes to encourage mothers everywhere through her humor, inspiration, and faith.

BONUS #5

A Word on Venting ...

By Michelle Nahom

Venting is natural. Back in the days of our childhood, our moms vented to their friends and neighbors. The neighborhood was an important part of their social being. Nowadays, many more moms work outside (or inside) the home, and the neighborhood isn't as much a part of our social fabric. We're busy carting kids to organized activities after a full day's work. We're not visiting at the bus stop or doing neighborhood potlucks. Sometimes we don't even really know our neighbors.

Now with the rise of the Internet, social media sites, and blogging, people are using those avenues to vent instead. So what used to be private (or semi-private anyway), we now shout out to the world on Facebook, Twitter, and our blogs. We complain about everything from our family to our life to our jobs, in a very public forum, where it's searchable … forever.

We're constantly telling our children to be careful what they put on the Internet. It can affect their college applications, their future jobs—one stupid post can haunt them until eternity.

But we don't practice what we preach. How many times have you seen someone complain about their job or their boss on Facebook or Twitter? You might not be Facebook friends with your boss, but your co-worker that you're friends with might be. There's a chance that your boss might see the post because your co-worker commented on it. Your co-worker might even mention it to her. Now think about your family. Do you have teenagers? They probably drive you nuts sometimes. Maybe you have a difficult relationship with another family member. When you write about these very private and difficult issues on social media, I guarantee they will see it at some point.

Relationships make up the fabric of our lives. Sometimes those difficult ones hang by a thread at times … a thread that can snap easily. In an instant, a relationship can change. Even if whatever you wrote was 100 percent true, *was it worth it?*

It feels good to vent. It feels good to say it out loud and get it off our chests. But maybe … just maybe … sometimes you'd be better off not putting it online.

The Holiday Meltdown

By Marie Bollman
Make Your Own Damn Dinner

Meltdowns come in all shapes and sizes. Most often mine involve yelling, cursing, crying, and door slamming. But this is the story of a different kind of meltdown. It's the story of the time I became so overwhelmed with motherhood and life in general, I did something I had never done before. And thankfully, I haven't done it since. It's the story of the worst holiday havoc that went down in history.

Let me take you back to Christmas time 2006—the most wonderful time of the year. My two sons are three years and eight months old. My hands are full with the usual holiday hustle and bustle. And, of course, the week before Christmas, my oldest son gets sick. (Point of reference: this kid doesn't just get sick. He gets SICK. And it almost always ends with an asthma flare up, resulting in a nasty cough.) Every mom knows that the holidays are stressful enough without having sick kids to take care of. I'm not going to lie, my stress level is high. Thankfully, by Christmas Eve he's well enough to go to my parents' house to celebrate with family. And even if he's not feeling great … maybe we just don't have to mention it. Nobody will ever know. Or so I thought.

The festivities are in full swing. Christmas music fills the air. My entire extended family is seated at my mom's elegant dining room table enjoying a delicious Christmas Eve dinner. We're talking ornate table cloths, linen napkins, fancy serving dishes, and even salad forks. *All the things I never use at home.* Everything is picture perfect. Perfect, that is, until my three-year-old starts having a coughing fit. He coughs and coughs. In fact, he coughs until his hacks turn into heaves. Finally he barfs all over his dinner plate. It's a true spectacle in front of aunts, uncles, cousins, and grandparents. It's times like these when I'm thankful my family has a great sense of humor. But that's not much of a consolation as I'm staring down at my mom's fancy table cloth covered in regurgitated Christmas spaghetti. I'm mortified! And I have no way of knowing that this is only the beginning of the fiasco yet to come.

The rest of the day passes without incident, unless you count getting made fun of relentlessly by my family. We keep my oldest sequestered, because the last thing we want to do is get everyone else sick. We all enjoy a wonderful evening together, but it's getting late. Time to get the kids to bed … Santa comes tonight! Since we are staying at my parents' house, we are about to put them in the direct path of our storm. We put both boys to bed and Mom and I sneak out to go to a Christmas Eve church service. Feeling relaxed and completely in the Christmas spirit, we come home to find my husband and my dad leaning over the washing machine trying to figure out how it works. All I hear is, "Well, it's shit, so we want to wash it in the hottest water possible." Um, excuse me. Whose shit? My eight-month-old's shit, of course. Apparently, while I was at church he woke up with some explosive diarrhea, which had leaked all over himself and his crib. Fantastic! This should make for a fun Christmas morning.

I spend the next half hour cleaning up human feces and grumbling to myself. All of a sudden my husband emerges from the bathroom to inform me he has been struck by a holly jolly double whammy, diarrhea AND vomiting. His face is the color of a corpse and he looks like he's on death's door. Are you kidding me?! Now I have to take care of two sick kids, a sick husband,

AND be ready for Christmas morning in a few hours? This can NOT be happening. The most wonderful time of the year, my ass!

At this point I'm feeling overwhelmed. I'd say frazzled is an understatement. It's the middle of the night and I'm physically and mentally exhausted. After the clean up is complete, I move on to playing Santa, getting the stockings stuffed, and the presents under the tree all by myself. I'm ready to sit down, devour Santa's cookies and milk, and cry out of sheer exasperation. I can FEEL the meltdown coming on. But I soldier on. It's what moms do, isn't it? My husband heads downstairs for a glass of water just as I'm heading upstairs to check on my kids. As we pass each other on the stairs it becomes obvious to me that he's feeling worse than I even thought. He has a fever and extreme body aches. And all that seems like nothing compared to his frequent and acute vomiting and diarrhea. (TMI? Sorry.)

I check in on my boys, who are nestled all snug in their beds, both sleeping peacefully and quite unaware of the chaos that is about to ensue. At least *someone* was enjoying a silent night. Uh oh. Suddenly, I'm feeling weak. And also a little light-headed. I'm not even positive I can make it back downstairs to finish getting ready for tomorrow morning. But I have to. Who else is going to do it if I don't? I'm at the top of the stairs looking down, and I'm feeling dizzy. *What is going on?* One foot at a time. One stair. Another stair. Uh oh, another stair. Wait. Why is the room spinning? Why am I sweating? I better sit down. Why is the world going black? What can I do? I know. I'll call my mom. She's sleeping in the next room. "Mom? Mom?" She springs from her bed to see what is the matter, unaware that I'm about to cause a large clatter—The Night Before Christmas style. "Mom? I think something's wrong." And with that, I'm out like a light.

Now this is the part of the story that I have no recollection of, due to the fact that I was unconscious. But it has been retold so often that it is now the stuff of legend. I just happen to be wearing satin pajamas. (Get your mind out of the gutter, people;

nothing slinky or sexy. Just long pants and long-sleeve, button-down pajamas.) So naturally, as soon as I faint, I start sliding down the stairs. My husband is down at the bottom of the stairs, feebly trying to make his way back up to bed. He's so weak he can hardly stand up, much less rush to my aid at the top of the stairs. That leaves it all up to my mom. She springs into action, grabbing me under the armpits to keep me from sliding all the way down the stairs. Since I'm not exactly elfish at 5' 10", she's using all her strength to hold me. And it's then that the fart sneaks out. Yep. Standing there in her night gown, clutching me, struggling to keep me from sliding into certain death, desperately calling for my dad to come help, my mom lets one rip. Yuletide flatulence, right there in front of her son-in-law! If I have a single regret from this entire ordeal, it's only that I wasn't awake to hear it for myself.

Several silent seconds pass. At last I'm coming to. My ears are ringing, but I'm starting to hear voices again. I prop myself up on a step and look to my left. *Why is my husband clinging to the railing and dragging himself up the stairs?* I look behind me. *Why is my dad standing on the landing in his underwear? And why is my mom so out of breath? Is she blushing?!*

You won't believe this, but the holiday hubbub doesn't end there. Let's cut to the next morning. Merry Freaking Christmas! Santa came and there's a big breakfast cooking, even though only a few of us feel well enough to eat it. We all gather around the tree to open presents. But, where's Papa? Almost as if on cue, the door to the garage opens and my dad drags himself inside. "Don't go out in the garage," he says pitifully. He looks awful! And judging by the chunks he blew all over the garage floor, this is the most contagious, rapidly spreading flu in the history of all sickness. We force ourselves to open presents, trying to ignore the fact that five out of six of us are feeling lousy. This is not the perfect holiday I had in mind. It's quite possibly the worst Christmas ever. I don't know if there has ever been a time when I have felt so much guilt. So we pack our bags and leave my

parent's house with our heads hanging. Our work here is done. *Or is it?*

In the week following our historic holiday havoc, the chain of people we infected went as follows: my sister-in-law, niece, and nephew got sick on Christmas Day (while they were at my sister-in-law's parent's house). They gave it to her parents, as well as their cousins on that side, who gave it to their mom (my sister-in-law's sister-in-law), who gave it to my sister-in-law's sister-in-law's mother, who said it was the sickest she's EVER been. God only knows who caught it from there. At some point it's just best to stop keeping track. And if you followed that twisting chain of germ infection, you deserve a prize. *Fruit cake, perhaps?*

So what's the moral of the story? Never, ever, EVER, under any circumstances bring your sick child to a family gathering and assume nobody has to know they're not feeling well. It just might result in a plague of epidemic proportions, with you blacked out and sliding down the stairs, which I can assure you, you will never live down. Almost seven years have passed since our holiday from hell, and we still reminisce about it often. The entire ordeal has become legendary in our family. Little did I know then, my mother of all meltdowns would ultimately become the gift that keeps on giving, in so many ways. Here's wishing you and yours a meltdown-free holiday season.

Marie Bollman is a former Special Education teacher turned SAHM. She lives in Minnesota with her husband and three kids, ages nine, seven, and four. She's a well-caffeinated, music loving, reality TV watching, political junkie who adores her family, but HATES cooking for them all. Rather than cleaning her house, she blogs about muddling her way through motherhood at Make Your Own Damn Dinner.

A Vacation Story

By Jennifer West
PinkWhen

*H*ave you ever had a meltdown because someone you didn't know crashed your vacation? As I was deciding which of my MANY meltdowns to share, I was able to easily narrow it down to this one. But, before I get into the meltdown portion of my little story, let me share with you a little about our family dynamics.

My husband and I have a blended family. When we got married, I had a daughter and he had two boys. We soon added our own little one to the mix, and the five of us became six. It's been quite the undertaking to go from one to four, and vacations sometimes seem more like a constant chore.

This past summer we took all the children to what we hoped would become our annual family vacation spot. Some people like to visit a new place every year, but we decided that we wanted to create lasting memories, as well as a tradition. We vacationed at the same spot the prior year when our youngest child was only one and hoped to continue the tradition for many years to come.

One of my husband's friends owns a house on the beach in a quaint little town called Navarre in Florida. It's a beautiful area with white sandy beaches, plenty of space, and not a lot of vacationers. We can literally walk from the house, down a short little boardwalk, and lounge on our own private beach. *Sounds like a little slice of heaven, right?* There are beautiful white beaches.

The blue water is crystal clear. Dolphins dance in the surf nearby. The vacation house is three-stories that sleeps fourteen. And your perfect little "Brady Bunch" family is there to share it all. *What is there to complain about?*

The beach is a long, ten-hour drive from where we live. The drive does not make for a fun time with five kids in the vehicle and two still in diapers. Oh, I said five! That's because the oldest daughter needed to have someone who is closer in age to play and hang out with. This part was actually good because her friend is a tad older, very mature, and has done a little light babysitting for us at home.

So let's talk about our vehicle for a moment. A few years ago we had to upgrade my husband's little sports car to a more suitable vehicle that can carry our bunch. We now have an SUV that can seat seven, with little wiggle room beyond that. To make the most out of a vacation such as this, you MUST have a hitch haul attached and try to keep the older girls from packing their entire rooms to bring along with them. Everyone was allowed one backpack. Whatever you could fit in the backpack you could bring, but everything else had to stay home. We had a washer and dryer at the beach house, so a lot of clothes was unnecessary.

I had to give you a little backup before I could just "dive right in." The meltdown was during the first twenty-four hours of this trip. This story isn't just about my meltdown; it's about others who had meltdowns, too. You're probably thinking, "Seven people in a car for ten hours is enough to make anyone have a meltdown." You'd be right. It would, at least if anything, drive a person to drink ... heavily.

After ten hours, we finally arrived at our destination and stopped at the rental company to pick up the keys. We were a little early and the house wasn't ready yet. We packed everyone back into the car and headed out to eat a late lunch. Not only was it hard to find a table for seven at any restaurant, but it was also expensive to feed seven people. Longing for the beach, we were stuck in a small restaurant with five stir-crazy kids and it

was raining. Not the best way to start a beach vacation, but I was still trying to be optimistic. Until …

My husband piped up and mentioned that a friend of his "might" be coming in tonight and would like to spend a day or two with us. My husband had an offshore fishing trip scheduled for a few of the older kids and the friend wanted to tag along. That was all okay, a little of an inconvenience, but I wasn't really bothered by it until I found out that his friend had picked up an unknown girlfriend on the way. This meant we now had two guests, an extra bed to clean, and two extra mouths to feed. Commence the grumblings of a possible meltdown.

After lunch we checked into our awesome house and let the kiddos run and stretch. The rain stopped, and on the balcony we could see forever. While marveling at the water and beautiful beach, we spotted a pod of dolphins jumping and playing in the water. The clouds started to break, and we saw little patches of blue sky and the sun peeking out. I was starting to feel like the day could be salvaged after all! While the kiddos were running around picking out rooms and we unpacked, I decided to leave and go to the grocery store. Feeding two adults and five kids is expensive, and now we had two more adult mouths to feed. I was wondering how I would manage to fit that into one buggy, let alone push the thing. Well, that's another story for another day.

When I returned, I unpacked the groceries and met everyone down at the beach. We enjoyed a lazy afternoon with partly cloudy skies and watched the kids all play in the surf. My husband's friends had not yet arrived, and we weren't expecting them in until later that night. We enjoyed a wonderful first day on the beach and a delicious meal on our first night of the annual family vacation. It was the best night of the vacation, because it all went downhill from there.

My husband's friend and his lady friend showed up at 10:00 p.m. Because the littlest one had an early bedtime and now had to sleep with us because of the extra guests, I turned in early. I didn't see everyone until morning.

That morning the little one woke up rather early. I walked downstairs to see who else was up and started working on breakfast. As I started rummaging through the fridge, I noticed a lot of extra items that I hadn't brought into the house. There was pineapple juice, vodka, rum, beer, beer, and more beer. While I don't mind a little bit of beer and fruity drinking at the beach, it looked like we had a bar brewing in our beach house. It was a little disturbing, but I tried to put it out of my mind. As I started making breakfast, everyone started to wake up and come downstairs to eat. I met my husband's friend and his guest, and everything seemed great.

Once breakfast was over, everyone started gearing up to go down to the beach. My husband and his friend began erecting a tent on the beach, and I grabbed all of the kiddos to take them to play before lunch. It was a beautiful sunny morning and everything seemed just fine. As I was sitting in my beach chair and watching the kids play in the surf and hunt for seashells, our guests came down and brought their drinks. At 9:00 a.m. Yep, 9:00 a.m.

Not wanting to be a party pooper, I didn't say anything, but I also don't drink anything besides Gatorade and water. I had a little premonition of how this day was going to turn out, and unfortunately my little "feelings" always turn out correct.

By the time 10:30 a.m. rolled around, our friend's girlfriend obviously had a little too much to drink. She was a very outgoing gal, but she was also a little tipsy. (Note to self, never do this around anyone or anyone you will ever see again.) I am not a big fan of the kiddos being around this, so I calmly walked them back up for a little rest from the heat and to eat an early lunch. After we ate lunch and the little one took a nap on the couch, I walked back down to the beach to check on all of the adults. Needless to say, it was now a little "hairier" than it was before I went up.

While the guys had also been drinking beer out in the sun, they decided it was cool to put on OIL. Not sunscreen—OIL.

Yep, OIL. The girlfriend apparently didn't like beer, so she stuck with the pineapple juice and rum. She had passed out in her chair, and woke up every once in a while to flash a boob at us. Not cool. However, I had yet to have my meltdown. *Can you believe that?* Not yet. I tried my best to sit and enjoy the sun while I waited for the older girls to come back down the walkway with news of the little one waking up. It didn't take too long, and when they walked back up I grabbed my husband and impolitely asked him to please walk with me.

At this point I was starting to lose my cool. What kind of example was this setting for the kids? I know my husband wanted to hang out with his friend, but his friend needed to walk his girlfriend back to the house for a shower and some Advil. She was obviously going to need it. We decided that my husband and his friend were going to pick up dinner at a great little seafood restaurant, and I was going to stay and watch the kids and our guest.

As I went back down to the beach with the children to watch them play, our guest remained passed out in a semi-dressed state. Nothing profane, but things *were* on the verge of falling out. Not to mention, she was wasted and she'd been baking in the sun all day. I was really starting to get pissed the more I sat and watched. This was supposed to be our family vacation, not a vacation bomb, and that's what it was slowly turning into.

The kids continued to play and have fun until almost 5:00 p.m. The guys were headed back from the restaurant, and I grabbed the kiddos to go back upstairs to clean up. Right as I was about to wake our sleeping guest, she suddenly woke up on her own. Obviously not feeling well from the hours of drinking and baking in the sun, she started to vomit over the side of her lounge chair. After she did this a few times, I finally lost my cool. I was now REALLY pissed. She started covering her vomit with the sand, and then laid back down to rest. That's it! I was now ROYALLY pissed! I headed upstairs, met my husband and his friend, and gave them an earful of exactly what I thought.

This was a family vacation, not Girls Gone Wild and wasted! Someone needed to go get her and bring her in from the beach. I was upset, my husband was upset, the friend was looking sheepish, and then our female guest graced us with her presence. She headed up the stairs without a word and was not seen again until the morning … the morning they left!

That's right. They did not stay another night. My husband went fishing with the kids the next day and things were starting to look up. We enjoyed our first full-day at the beach with the family, and my husband put a ton of sunscreen all over his crazy sunburned body.

While I know that "stuff" happens, I was still about to boil over from the events of the past twenty-four hours of our vacation. There are a few key takeaways from this little scenario. Do not drink liquor at 9:00 a.m. unless you are used to it. Do not put sunbathing oil on your body unless you have a base tan, and probably not even then. Do not pass out in the sun. And, under no circumstances, ever, get so drunk that you start flashing your boobs at people you barely know. Covering the puke in the sand was probably the best thing that happened.

Jennifer West is a southern girl living in Louisiana, who is addicted to crafting. When she sees something she likes, she has this crazy need to try to make it. With her blog, PinkWhen, she gets to share all of the addiction of DIY, crafting, upcycling, recipes, healthy living, and more. She and her husband have four kiddos that they merged together to become quite the little "Brady Bunch." They have two girls, ages twelve and two years old, and two boys, who are eight and five. Needless to say, they stay quite busy!

Stranger Than Avocados

By Andrea Moore
BeQuoted

"**W**hy don't you just answer her?!" It was more of a demand than a question.

Our Father who art in heaven … Quickly I began a silent recitation of the prayer so familiar to me that I didn't even need to think about the words. I decided to use them as a floating device, because surely I was about to drown.

The Lord's Prayer is my safety net. I use it to bring me calm and tranquility, to take my mind off the pain of a bikini wax, or during unexpected moments like this—to keep me from pouncing on the woman who has made the horrible decision to yell for me to answer my three-year-old who was crying and shouting, "Mommy! Mommy!" as I casually strolled down the produce aisle reaching for an avocado. By the way, this avocado would have actually propelled quite the distance should I have turned around and thrown it at the woman yelling for me to "just answer her!"

But I'm getting ahead of myself.

It was Cinco de Mayo weekend. Attempting to be a good wife and mother, I decided we'd have a festive meal of fish tacos topped with mango salsa. I had the list of ingredients stuffed in my huge bag-like-luggage right next to my daughter's fold-up potty seat cover and Clorox wipes. Lip gloss, potty seat, wallet, and list of ingredients. That was all I needed for our trip to the grocery store. Had I known I was going to be bullied by a lady wearing sweats in 89-degree weather, I would have also packed a retractable dustpan to use once I cleaned the floor with this woman—but I digress.

At the stop light waiting to make a left turn into the busy parking lot, my daughter noticed that we were headed toward one of her most hated places—anywhere there is a shopping cart, a seat, and a seat belt, USA. Immediately she said, "Mommy, no shopping cart." As if! It was three in the afternoon. She and I had been running errands since ten that morning without a nap break in between. We were both on edge. Before we got out of the parked car, I turned to my little one for a quick pow-wow and semi-bribe, "When we get inside the store you're getting into the shopping cart. Mommy is going to grab a few items, and then we'll leave so that we can get chicken nuggets, fries, and apple juice. Understand?" (I never say *okay* to my daughter because I don't want her to think for even one second that I'm asking her permission, but Lawd do I wish she would have granted permission on that day.) She looked at me tearfully and repeated, "No shopping cart."

Damn. I'll make it quick, I decided. In and out and we'd all live happily ever after. Yes. That's what would happen. After all, little girls are made up of "sugar and spice and everything nice." What a bunch of bull. On the basis of false advertisement, I'm actually looking to sue the person who wrote that little nursery rhyme.

I struggled to get Little One's long, wiggling legs into the shopping cart. All the while she cried and repeated her grocery store mantra, "No shopping cart. Mommy? No shopping cart." I hadn't even made it to the groceries yet and already she was at the tipping point of what would be an epic meltdown. I pulled her in for a hug, rubbed her back, and whispered, "Mookie," yes, I call her that and a host of other nicknames she'll one day be too embarrassed to answer to, "we'll get some nuggets and fries after you sit in the shopping cart while Mommy gets just a few items.

It won't take long." It wouldn't. It wasn't like I was in Target or some other cult-like shopping bonanza.

She continued to whine, then full-out cry, never breaking away from her mantra-on-repeat. I reiterated that she was to stay in the shopping cart. She was tired and irritated. I too had grown quite weary and agitated at this point. I stopped answering her because my answer was not going to change. As a mommy, I make it a point not to feed into my daughter's every demand, especially when she's whining and throwing a temper tantrum. In my world, if I had taken her out of the shopping cart, she would have learned that in order to get Mommy to do what I want all I have to do is create a scene and have a meltdown. That is not the message I wanted her to receive. I decided not to answer her any more. I just rubbed her little hands as I looked straight ahead pushing the cart and pretending that the other shoppers weren't paying us any attention. I told Little One in the car and twice in the store that she wasn't getting out of the shopping cart. That was final. Lady in the sweats hadn't got the memo and decided to offer up some unsolicited parenting advice served with irritation as an appetizer and disgust for dessert, "Why don't you just answer her?!"

I didn't even make it to the middle of the Lord's Prayer before I whipped my head around and asked this woman to excuse herself. I refused to explain to this stranger that my child was sleepy and that answering her would not stop her from crying and asking me to let her out of the shopping cart. I refused to explain to this stranger that children—and mothers— have meltdowns and that I was not going to carry my thirty-five pound child through the store while I shopped for tortilla shells and tomatoes. I refused! I lost it. I tried so hard not to lose my cool, especially in public and in front of my snotty-nosed, crying child, but this lady had lost her mind and I too had lost mine in the process.

I think the sliding doors at the EXIT and ENTRANCE of the grocery store may have actually slid closed, the red emergency warning lights blared, and a neon sign had replaced the name of the grocery store with blinking lights that read: "Warning: Meltdown in 5, 4, 3, 2 …"

My body temperature had become dangerously hot, or was the air conditioner broken? I was entering into a mommy meltdown first, and quite possibly entering into the back of a police car next. Who would pick my daughter up from the precinct? I'd have to worry about that on my ride in the back of the squad car. Right now I was morphing into another being and literally melting under the glare of the grocery store lights, what felt like a million stares, shear embarrassment, and the audacity of this woman! Little One took my cue as consent to sink further into her own meltdown and continued to bawl, and yes, shout between sobs, "No shopping cart!" *Was this happening?* It was.

Lady in the sweats and I exchanged a few words. My words were leaving my mouth much faster than hers were (attribute that to my mommy ability to multi-task), with me ending the conversation with, "Mind your business. If you have such a huge problem with a toddler's crying, feel free to visit your nearest adults-only grocery store." Humph. Clean up in the produce aisle!

Still in the throes of an epic meltdown and blinded by the smoke permeating my ears, it took me longer than usual to notice that the lady in sweats had disappeared to presumably meddle in someone else's parenting affairs. I was no longer feeling festive or like a good ole' wife and mother. I took my sleepy, crying daughter out of the shopping cart—her desire from the very beginning—and left the store empty handed and silently reciting …

And forgive us our trespasses, as we forgive those who trespass against us. Lead us not into temptation …

Andrea S. Moore is a San Francisco born and raised freelance writer and social work healthcare clinician. She is the editor-in-chief of BeQuoted, where she frequently blogs about self-acceptance and self-esteem, parenting, education, marriage and relationships, humor, and healthcare. She lives in Virginia with her husband and daughter.

When Meltdowns are Necessary: Raising a Strong Woman and Not a Tough Broad

By Kristen Daukas
Four Hens and a Rooster

I was raised in a relatively emotionless family.

We didn't cry.

We didn't shout.

We hardly raised our voices and, looking back on it, there wasn't a lot of boisterous laughter either.

Everything was always middle of the road okay—even when it wasn't. I was never really allowed to express my opinion, much less an opinion with emotion. My parents never fought and if they had problems, the only way that I would have ever picked up on that was by the quiet walks they took down the hall and the quiet whispers behind their bedroom door. As a self-involved teenager, I'm surprised even that caught my attention.

By the time I was a junior in high school, I was never home. I was part of an exclusive high school drama program that met each day for a class that was two hours long, but in actuality, because of our high volume of productions, lasted at least until 6:00 p.m. each day. I honestly think the reason I loved drama and the theatre so much was because there was absolutely none of it in my life, and I was finally given the room to let it all hang out. My parents loved me without question, but we just weren't the lovey, touchy, vocal type of family.

Understand this isn't to say that I've lived life without witnessing or having a few good meltdowns. There was the time that I found out my first real high school boyfriend thought two southern belles were better than one (and one with a name like Dixie, no less). And there was the time I discovered that my roommate of thirty-five days was nothing short of a certified nut job (that one ended with a covert move-out in the middle of the night) and a few others before, between, and after.

Did we have meltdowns when the girls were little? Sure. Did they lose their minds because they couldn't have yet another piece of crap toy in the store? Or a certain kind of cookie instead of the one that I just put in front of them? Did at least two of them have some crazy aversion to seams in their socks and would run screaming if I gave them "those" socks? Absolutely. But honestly, they were becoming just like their mother ... tough little cookies with a rock solid outside.

When people tell you that children learn what they live— believe them. I encourage them to speak their minds and say what they feel, but at the same time, I've taught them to "never let them see you cry" especially when it comes to dealing with mean girls and bullies.

At this point of our lives, meltdowns actually take work on my part. But sometimes, it just has to happen.

When you know your kids, you know when things aren't right. And when things aren't right, they're not right and the whole balance of the house is off. Whatever balance may exist in a house that includes one teen and two tweens.

For the 2013-2014 school year, we have the luxury of having a girl in each school. One in elementary, one in middle school, and one in high school. I can do the elementary school agenda and back-to-school with my eyes closed and the same with middle school. But this is the first year for high school. I've been reading about the school and the teachers. I've sought out all of their Twitter accounts and followed them. I've copied all the calendars to mine, and I was as excited for freshman orientation

as she was. Maybe more so.

The day of orientation, I was up, making breakfast (unheard of activity in this house in the middle of the week), and excited to take her and her friend to drop them off for their full day of orientation or, really, an actual day "run through." I listened and TOOK NOTES during the parent portion of the day, and I couldn't wait for her to get home to hear all about her teachers, who was in her class, and what her schedule was going to be.

Basically, I was setting myself up for heartbreak.

When we met up after parent orientation, instead of the bouncing, happy teenager (wait, does that even exist outside of my head?), I was met with the expressionless face of a teen girl who'd rather eat raw chicken liver than be there with her parents.

Any and all questions about her day were met with the same three expressionless responses given out in rotation, "Fine." "Whatever." "I don't know." I shook it off and credited it to the "cool kid" attitude and shuttled the posse out the door to get ready for the second part of the day—back-to-school night.

You know the old saying "insanity is doing the same things the same way and expecting different results?" If you haven't learned that lesson yet as a parent, you will when you hit the double digits.

Later that day, we returned for the second portion of freshman orientation. This is the part of the day where you get to meet teachers and walk through their daily schedule, and yes, friends, I was just as excited for this piece as I was for the earlier piece.

And yes, friends, I was met with the same results.

Instead of getting to spend a few minutes with each teacher and the three of us getting to exchange names and handshakes, we were given the whiplash, drive-by tour with a fourteen-year-old driver at the helm on the roughest ocean possible. She still was unfamiliar with the halls, so we laughed when we went down the same hall three times and, of course, the interpretation was that we were laughing at her. After three failed attempts at meeting her homeroom teacher and being treated like a second-class citizen, I finally had enough and announced that I was done and leaving and proceeded out the front door with the Rooster in tow and gape-mouthed teenager looking at the back of my head.

By the time we got to the car, I had received the "in shock" texts begging us to come back; that she had found her homeroom teacher and (now) she wanted us to meet him.

I didn't budge, because the only reason it was important to her now was because she knew that she had pushed me too far.

As the door slammed to announce her arrival, I said nothing. I waited until we were driving and in that calm voice which means "you've gone too far" I let her know how upset I was and then I started to cry. I explained to her how excited I had been to share this day with her. How much I looked forward to her coming home and telling me about her day and all the great parts of it. How much her dad and I looked forward to going back with her and meeting her teachers and yes—even though her dad told corny jokes and tried to befriend all her teachers and pals—it was a big night for him, too.

"And you ruined it for both of us."

By the time we reached the house, I had pulled myself together but the other two knew something wasn't right. I was still at that fragile point that if I thought about the incident, I would start crying again. The middle was trying to figure out what had happened and stopped cold in the kitchen when she saw the tears. "I have never seen you cry, Mommy," my twelve-year-old said, as she wrapped me in a hug.

I find the Rooster and tell him that while I'm upset, there's just something not right about the entire situation. Sure, she was mean and unpleasant but even on her worst days, she's not this bad. There's something else going on. As we're having this conversation, the middle returns to the scene, but with a much different game face on. This is the face of the defender. Out of desperation and a desire to save face, the oldest has enlisted her younger sister to fight her battle.

And the house begins to shake.

It's not her fault that I'm upset, but rather our fault for forcing her into doing things she doesn't want to do—awful things such as being on the golf team. "But you LIKE playing golf and you were EXCITED to be on the team," we say.

"NO! I hate golf and I hate playing and this entire year is going to SUCK because of you."

"THEN QUIT! Quit the team and spend your entire year playing the sport of socializing, because THAT will get you so far in life" I argue. "There is something going on with you that you are NOT telling me because I cannot believe that you are THIS upset over the concept of playing a team sport."

And just like that, the final straw breaks and she crumbles into the pool of an emotional meltdown.

It turns out that the kid that she had spent four weeks going out with had started spreading rumors. In the realization that she was never getting back together with him, he did what many insecure boys do and started talking smack.

This is a kid that I had pegged from the beginning as being insecure and controlling, and I watched over them like a hawk. She told me I was crazy and that it wasn't true but as adults, we KNOW what controlling and possessive looks like, and as the mother to daughters, I will go to my grave to keep them from getting in one of those relationships.

But it took this mammoth meltdown between us for her to finally see what I had seen for months. He may be a nice kid to everyone else, but not to you. "You do not have to take this," I tell her. "You've been apart four times longer than you were together. If he's doing this to you, you need to block him from your life."

"But I can't! Everyone is going to believe him, because he's on the football team and now my school year is ruined!"

"No. Your year will not be ruined," I say.

"What can you do about it? Tell his mother? You can't do that!"

"The hell I can't tell his mother," I say. "I will tell his mother, his father, the school counselor … I will tell anyone and everyone that will listen and do something because you are my daughter and it is my job to protect you! I've taught you to handle many things, but this is one of those that you cannot do on your own and you must let us know when something like this happens."

As a parent it is so easy for us to know why kids act the way they do. It's almost textbook with the ones that cause problems. And I feel for the kids that have these issues and baggage they carry around. But I don't care enough to let it affect my family and the mental well-being of my daughters. It is my job to raise three independent, self-reliant, strong women, and nothing or no one will stand in my way. Not even them. And if I have to push some buttons on them to help me break down that wall that I taught them to build, I'll do it.

So see, sometimes meltdowns aren't a bad thing.

Kristen Daukas was born and raised in Greensboro, North Carolina, but has lived in Chicago (three times), Vail, and the 'burbs of Philly. She currently lives with her family in Winston-Salem, North Carolina, a place she hopes to stay for a long, long time—unless an unexpected lottery win affords her the opportunity to retire in the Caribbean. She is the mother to three active daughters aged fifteen, twelve, and ten, and the wife to one very patient man. Rounding out their chaotic lives is one dog and one cat. Kristen started her foray into blogging back in 2003 when she and the family lived in Pennsylvania. The launch of Four Hens and a Rooster happened because, with three young kids, she really didn't have time to run to Walgreens to print off pictures to mail off to the family. In late 2011 Kristen launched another project, Ten to Twenty Parenting, which is a community site dedicated to parents with kids between the ages of ten and twenty years old. She was a top five finalist in 2012 for a Shorty Award for #1 Mom in Social Media.

The Great Powdered Sugar Fight of 2007

By Marcia Kester Doyle
Menopausal Mother

*E*very year when the holidays roll around, I expect the season to be as cheery as the Christmas scenes depicted in a Norman Rockwell painting: snowy sidewalks, bells ringing, carolers singing, and happy shoppers strolling down sidewalks. And every year the reality of the season hits me while I'm standing for thirty minutes in a Walmart line. Toddlers screaming. Tempers flaring. People who haven't bathed since Bush was in office. No Perry Como crooning Christmas songs of peace and love through the store stereo system … just Lil Wayne rapping about guns, money, and hoes.

In 2007, the Christmas holidays were more hectic than usual. I was running three school fundraisers simultaneously, working a second part-time job, and raising a houseful of teens. My husband was also putting in extra hours at work. The holidays exacerbated the stress levels we already faced by dumping additional responsibilities on everyone in the family.

I'll admit that I become like a drill sergeant during the holidays. Trapped in that Norman Rockwell mindset, I insist on sticking with the traditions I grew up with … Christmas festivities that always began in our home before the Thanksgiving turkey had grown cold.

It was no different in 2007, beginning with the unloading of twenty-five giant, Rubbermaid containers, filled with what my husband fondly referred to as "Christmas Crap." Once he saw all the boxes that were labeled "Assembly Required," he delved heavily into the spiked eggnog to bolster himself for the long month of December. We argued over the mass of tangled, outdoor lights, the blinking Santas, and the illuminated trees. By the time my husband had every blade of grass on the front lawn decorated in artificial lights, NASA could have spotted our home from outer space.

Adding to our tension was the jacked up credit card bills from the holiday shopping that we feared would cause us to take out a second mortgage on our home. The Christmas spending spree turned my husband into the Grinch and Scrooge all rolled into one.

On one particular evening when our patience had been pushed to the limit, I shooed my husband out the door with an extensive grocery list so that I could tackle the giant mound of cookie dough on the kitchen counter. One hundred cookies were due at the kid's schools the following morning. I thought of the hours of rolling and baking ahead of me and felt my blood pressure rise. *Where were all of Santa's elves when I needed them?* I already knew where my little elves were. They were playing video games, blasting rap music, and watching reality TV shows with their friends. Resentment simmered inside of me. I gritted my teeth and asked the teens to help me.

"Too busy right now!"

"I need to beat this next level on my game. Just give me a minute."

"Mom, can't you see that I'm on the phone?"

And that's when I flipped. I went from June Cleaver to Mommie Dearest in a nanosecond. The shrieking shrew with the crazed eyes was enough to make the teens jump off the couch and report for cookie duty. The batter had to be rolled into one hundred balls, baked, and dipped twice in powdered sugar. A long, arduous task, but the end result of sugary goodness was worth it. We worked like a factory assembly line—rolling,

baking, and dipping. It was a monotonous chore that I did with a clenched jaw and aching feet, from standing in the kitchen all day. Bags of powdered sugar lined the messy counter top. My oldest son was busy dipping the warm cookies in sugar when suddenly he looked up with a mischievous glint in his eyes. I recognized that look from before and nothing good ever came of it. It was then that he decided to make the mundane task more interesting by flinging a handful of powdered sugar at his friend's face. The poor girl just stood stunned, her face a white mask of sugar. She blinked in disbelief several times and small, powdery flakes sifted down from her eyelashes onto her cheeks. I had a very bad feeling about this.

Things quickly got out of hand once my son's friend decided to retaliate. It was as if someone sounded the alarm and all hell broke loose. Everyone frantically grabbed fistfuls of powdered sugar and began throwing it at one another. Like an energetic game of paintball, we dodged globs of sugar by jumping over furniture and crawling under tables. No room in the house was off limits. I ran for cover in my bedroom and locked the door. I leaned against the frame, my heart racing. *What the hell was going on?* My house was being systematically destroyed by demonic teenagers cracked out on Christmas cookies.

After a few minutes, the house fell eerily silent. Assuming my kids had come to their senses, I cracked open the door and tiptoed out. A battle cry that would have made Crazy Horse proud erupted from the hallway as five teenagers descended upon me, pelting me with balls of powdered sugar. By the time they had finished, I resembled Frosty the Snowman's evil twin.

As my blissfully ignorant husband was strolling down grocery aisles in search of guacamole and a good chardonnay, his family was engaged in powdered sugar warfare. We pummeled each other for half an hour, yelling and laughing until our sides ached. I stood back and blinked through the powdery haze. When Bing Crosby sang "White Christmas," I don't think he was referring to the artificial winter wonderland my teens and

I had created throughout the house. We were out of breath, our faces unrecognizable under layers of white powder. We looked like a deranged troupe of clowns from a dysfunctional circus.

It was at that moment that all the anger and stress from the holidays that I had bottled up inside, left my body. I laughed so hard at the pale faces around me that I had tears in my eyes. THIS was how my family relieved stress.

The phone suddenly rang, jarring me from my happy reverie. It was my husband calling to say he'd be home soon from the grocery store. Panicked, I surveyed the snowy mess we'd made and barked out cleaning orders. Everyone scattered like ants near a can of Raid. We swept and mopped and vacuumed as if we were amped up on Red Bull, racing against the clock.

By the time my husband arrived, our faces were scrubbed and the house was sparkling clean. When everyone gathered around the dining room table for supper, I noticed little white particles sifting down from my son's left earlobe and had to stifle a chuckle.

Years later, while moving furniture around the living room, I found a small dusting of confectioner's sugar behind the couch. It reminded me that life is too short to hold onto anger, especially if you're trapped in a Walmart line with a cart full of LED Christmas gnomes.

The moral of the story: Don't let stress control your temper. Flip on the humor switch and roll with the punches … or buy a bag of confectioner's sugar and start your own powder war.

Marcia Kester Doyle is the author of the humorous blog Menopausal Mother, where she muses on the good, the bad, and the ugly side of menopausal mayhem. Give her some wine and a jar of Nutella and she'll be your best friend. Marcia's work has appeared on Scary Mommy, In the Powder Room, The Erma Bombeck Writer's Workshop, Mamapedia, Bloggy Moms, Messy Mom's Radio, The Woven Tale Press, the Life Well Blogged series, and she was voted a Top 25 blogger in the 2013 Circle of Moms Contest.

When Meltdowns Collide

By Crystal Ponti
MommiFried

*L*ife really is an unexpected journey, as cliché as that sounds. Full of these huge ups and downs, it often gives us branches when we had hoped for the apple tree. My grandmother used to say, "Never expect life to work out exactly how you planned for it has a mind of its own." Boy, was she ever right.

My first big life lesson came at the age of seventeen, when I very unexpectedly found out I was pregnant. This may have been around the time that I had my first epic meltdown. We'll call it the pre-mother of all meltdowns. Standing in the middle of Planned Parenthood, I couldn't wrap my head around what I was hearing. Something about a positive result … that I would need to make a decision … that I had to eat well and take prenatal vitamins … *WHOA! WHAT?*

Forget vitamins! I'd been taking birth control as prescribed. There was NO way in hell I was with child. Clear as day, I remember all the blood rushing to my face and repeatedly asking the clinic technician to check the results again. When she declined because "these things are never wrong," I immediately lost my shiznit. This must have given her an opportunity to reflect on the situation and have a change of heart. Or maybe it was because twenty other girls around my age were so traumatized by my pungent reaction to pregnancy, they were forced to do damage control.

Either way, a second test and nine months later, a beautiful baby boy came into the world. We called him He-Who-Was-Miracle. No. We really named him Keith, because we were a little short on boys' names (major understatement). Two ultrasounds had previously revealed that a girl bun was in the oven; a girl we were going to call Samantha. Enter life unexpected.

When this tiny baby finally emerged, all our obstetrician could say was, "Ooops." For some strange reason "it" had a penis where a vagina was supposed to be. This time we were told that "these things [ultrasounds] are sometimes wrong." *You don't say?*

We had no boys names picked out, and right before leaving the hospital, it dawned on me that everything at home was pink. EVERYTHING! The crib bedding was adorned with cute, bubbly pink monkeys. The going home outfit was a velvety pink dress and bonnet. Even the damn thank you cards (that I had already started sending out) were a rosy shade of pink. *What happened?* Epic meltdown number two was underway. All I can say is thank the baby gods for receipts and unisex clothing. Keith rocked yellow like no kid before him.

Once we got through this hurdle, life was on the up. Aside from the eyeball rolling and so-called stereotyping that comes with being a teen mom, times were good. Being the Capricorn that I am, I was determined to prove to the world that I was every bit as ready to be a mom as the woman many years my senior.

Keith was an amazingly good baby, and I was instantly spoiled. Independent and strong-willed, he wanted to do for himself and get around on his own as soon as he was strong enough. He gave me the false impression that all babies were well-behaved little geniuses.

Two years later, I gave birth to my second lovey, another boy, Adam, and another momentous occasion. Despite the fact that Keith wanted to send him back and was devastated for a short time that he had competition vying for center stage, life was still on the up. For the twenty-four blissful months that followed,

I held my own. In some ways, I actually resembled Wonder Woman. I was proud! Why people made such a big fuss over motherhood was bewildering. For me, it was a walk in the park.

Then one day everything changed. My boys turned four and two. They went from being beautiful baby boys to holy outright terrors overnight! I was completely unprepared for this dramatic evolution, and it made me a little angry that no one thought to give me a heads up on how quickly things can change in this little game called parenthood.

Instead of gossiping about how I should have chosen a different path or pointing fingers at everyone in my life who was to blame for my young maternal age, someone should have stepped up and warned me that all children are different—and that some can be much more work than others. Hell. Someone should have just come right out and said, "Girl, you're in deep shit."

The days and months that followed were a mash up of Dennis the Menace moments and Evil Knievel stunts. On most days, I was run ragged. My boys were the equivalent of the Tasmanian Devil meets Bart Simpson. I loved them with all my heart and soul, but this motherhood stuff was no longer a simple, routine task. I had entered a circus ring that had somehow landed smack dab in the middle of a jungle burning to the ground.

Everything would come to a roaring head on a hot July evening. As long as I live, I'll never forget this day.

It started seven days prior after a trip to the grocery store. My mom was good enough to come along with me for moral support. When we got there, the boys were so wound tight we decided it might be better for her to sit in the vehicle and wait with them.

Like a good mom, I unstrapped them from their car seats, made sure the air conditioner was a comfortable temperature, and wished my dear mom good luck. When I returned from making a mad dash through the store, I noticed an older man leaning over the passenger side window speaking with my mom.

It was a family friend she hadn't seen in years, and I was glad she was having an opportunity to catch up. I also wondered if the boys were sleeping, because it was uncharacteristically quiet in the vehicle.

That's until I noticed a small crowd laughing hysterically as they walked by the back of my Chevy Blazer. Before I got there, several other couples had walked by, nearly falling over in hysterics. *What the hell was on the rear of my vehicle?*

As I rounded the back, it became immediately clear. There were two naked butts squished firmly against the back window. My endearing children had spent the better part of twenty minutes mooning the patrons of Hannaford Supermarket. My mother, chatting along, hadn't a clue.

When they caught sight of me, they knew instantly to pull their pants back up and run for their seats. I'll never know which one was a brighter shade of red, my face or their rear ends from the pressure of the glass being pressed so firmly against them.

The entire ride home I was shaking as I kept glancing at their silent bodies sitting perfectly in their seats. *Where did they learn such horrible behavior, and why ... why did it have to happen in a public place? Could they not have mooned my mother back at her house?* That I could have dealt with, probably with a laugh or two.

A few days later, the nightmare that was my two sons continued. Early on a Saturday morning, as I was busy cleaning the house, it once again became much too quiet. The normal screaming and tossing of blunt objects had ceased. With all the warning bells going off, I entered a crisp mode of panic when I couldn't find them anywhere in the house. I spent twenty minutes frantically looking for them outside when out of the corner of my eye, I saw something move in the distance.

We had recently built a small addition onto the back of the house. It was two stories high, intended for storage. There, running back and forth on the roof, were Taz and Bart. My stomach nearly fell to the ground. *How in the hell did they get up there? And how was I going to remain calm enough to coax them*

down? With no one there to help me, I dashed back inside.

At the end of the upstairs hallway, I noticed a window open in the back bedroom, and I could faintly see their little bodies bouncing up and down. The escape artists had managed to unlock the window and climb out onto the roof.

With my head now hanging out the window, I calmly asked them to come back inside. Outright refusal lead to concerned anger, if there is even such a thing. On one hand, I was furious they could misbehave in such a manner. On the other hand, I didn't give a bleep about them being naughty or nice. Their lives were on the line and that instantly trumped all else.

Thinking it was a game, they continued to bounce, run, and dash from side to side, not realizing the inherent dangers. That's when I got creative. I went to the kitchen and grabbed an entire bowl full of candy, something that was normally rationed out in small portions. Bribery wasn't in my nature, but I was ready to resort to anything to bring them to safety.

When they saw me dangling the bowl from the window, they dove back inside. They were like two little puppy dogs with their tongues hanging out. All I could do for what seemed like an eternity was crush them with hugs. I knew the candy would cause them to dance off the walls all night long, but it didn't matter. I let them engorge themselves until they were a fancy shade of green. Many people feel I rewarded them for their bad behavior. To them, I say "bite me." It was an act of desperation. And I was desperate to make sure they didn't plummet to their deaths. My kids. My choice. My good outcome.

It wasn't but a few days later when they would cause me to have yet another heart attack. Once again, things got awfully quiet in the house when I snuck a few minutes to go the bathroom. When I was done, a quick search confirmed what I had feared. They were gone! After searching high and low for approximately ten minutes, it occurred to me that the front door had been wide open when I went outside to look for them. It didn't click at the time, because I was in a sheer panic.

Just then, the house phone rang. It was my mother who, at the time, lived right down over the hill. In the milliseconds that I was taking a private pee, they had decided they were hungry and would venture to their grandmothers ALONE to fetch some food. Of course I was relieved, but I was also not taking a second chance on this happening again. A deadbolt was quickly added to the door, well out of reach from little hands.

Thinking my time of torture was surely over, I settled back into a comfort zone. BIG MISTAKE! The following night … that epic July evening … after returning home from work and cooking dinner, I hopped into the recliner to watch *Jeopardy*. The boys played Matchboxes nearby on the living room floor. All was right in the world until I accidentally fell asleep for fifteen minutes. I never dozed off while they were awake, because I knew the repercussions could be horrendous. The boys required constant watching and monitoring.

I awoke to Alex Trebek's voice and the sound of the Final Jeopardy theme song. But that's not all I woke up to find. Dazed and confused from the catnap, I instantly smelled the condiments reminiscent of an outdoor BBQ—the scent of mustard and ketchup filled the air. *Had my mother snuck in and cooked us another meal?* I wouldn't be so lucky.

After wiping the cobwebs from my eyes, it became clear what had happened in the few minutes that I had slept. The boys found squirt bottles of ketchup and mustard and proceeded to decorate my entire kitchen and living room—ceiling to floor. It had only been a few weeks prior when we officially finished the house, adding new carpets and fresh paint to the walls. The baby blue rugs and eggshell interiors now resembled a contemporary splatter painting.

My mother of all meltdowns came on without warning. As the boys, now covered in yellow and red goo, hovered in a corner, I fell to my knees. The ear-piercing, lunatic screech that I let out next could have been mistaken for an earthquake tremor. Instantly, my eyes welled up with tears, and I began to sob

uncontrollably. Fist-to-floor pounding followed. I must have looked like Muhammad Ali on a bad day. It was then that all mental emotions and bodily functions ceased. The crying stopped and not a sound could be heard as I stood up like a zombie had come to life. The crazed look in my eyes was enough to send both boys fleeing to their rooms. I was going to kill something! I was sure of it.

As I took several wild steps forward, two things occurred to me. First, I was to blame for the disaster. I fell asleep and ultimately left the boys unsupervised. And second, no matter what, no matter how angry and momentarily delusional I was, I loved them. Unconditionally.

Several deep breaths were in order, along with a call to my mother. When she walked into the house, she laughed. *What else could anyone do?* It looked like a hot dog stand had exploded. We spent the next several hours cleaning up little boys and a not-so-little mess.

When I look back on that day and that incredibly crazy week, I wonder how I survived without having a complete nervous breakdown. Clearly, youth was on my side twenty-somewhat years ago. If this had happened recently, there's no doubt my new home would be a padded cell prepped in bright white!

Crystal Ponti is a digital marketing consultant and online community expert who has worked for some of the largest sites in the world, including Answers.com and Google, among others. She is currently focused on helping authors market their books in the most efficient and productive ways possible—both on and offline. When she is not busy consulting, she can be found nurturing a beautiful family of five children, one much-younger husband, and a cat that drives them all up the wall. She started her blog MommiFried as an outlet for her creative writing and to share her later-in-motherhood experiences with all women and parents. Her work has been featured on BlogHer, The SITS Girls, and Business2Community, and she was recently named a Top 25 Foodie Mom for 2013 and a Top 25 Family Blog for 2012 by Circle of Moms.

BONUS #6

Meltdown Recovery
By Dana Hemelt

So you've had a meltdown. You temporarily transformed into Medusa, but you are now ready to tuck those snakes back under your cap and rejoin the civilized world. There are various things you can do to recover; pick the ones that work best for you.

Breathe. You probably stopped doing this at some point during your meltdown. *In for two, out for two. Again.* Feel your heartbeat and breathing slow to a normal rate. Wipe the sweat off your brow, reapply the deodorant, and change into a dry shirt.

Pour yourself a glass of wine, a beer, or a vodka tonic. If you prefer, have a cup of tea or coffee. Take slow sips and let the liquid soothe you. Eat some chocolate, too.

Distance yourself from the little people who have caused your meltdown. Not permanently, of course, but a temporary separation will facilitate recovery. This should only be done if there is another adult present or if it is legally permissible to leave the munchkins alone.

Take a hot bubble bath or shower. Let the water calm you, and stay in there until your fingertips are wrinkly.

Put on your ear buds and let the music do its magic. The tunes should make you chill to an almost comatose state. Try Kenny G., Yanni, or anything New Age.

Eat a turkey sandwich. Or anything else with tryptophan, like nuts or cheese. It works on all the men at Thanksgiving; it may work for you now.

Go for a run. Exercise can burn off the residual anger, and as a bonus, it will also burn off the calories from the wine and chocolate.

Watch an episode of Friends. Laughing will help relax you, and 99 percent of the episodes are completely child-free.

Forgive yourself. Meltdowns happen to the best of us.

Remember those stinkers who caused the meltdown in the first place? Snuggle with them, hug them, and kiss them. After the crisis, you are all in need of positive physical affection. Hug long and hard, and let them know that Mommy loves them even when she loses it.

16703757R00128

Made in the USA
Middletown, DE
20 December 2014